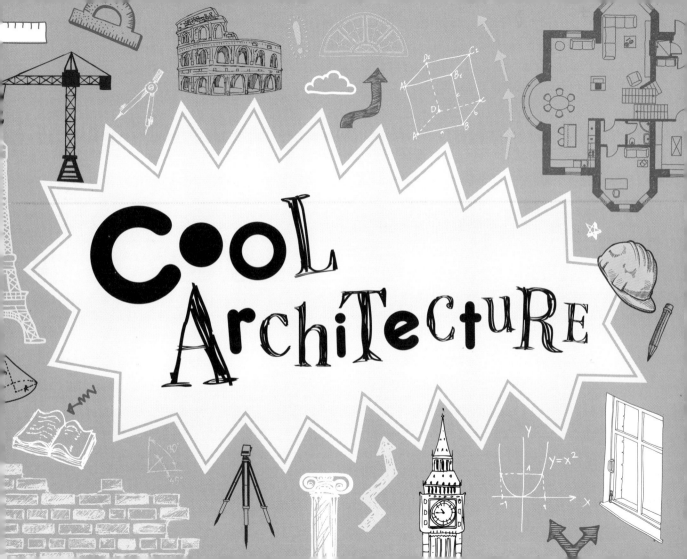

First published in the United Kingdom in 2015 by
Pavilion
43 Great Ormond Street
London
WC1N 3HZ

ISBN 978-1-90939-679-1

A CIP catalogue record for this book is available from the British Library.

10 9 8 7 6 5 4

Reproduction by Mission Productions Ltd, Hong Kong
Printed and bound by Times Offset (M) Sdn Bhd, Malaysia

This book can be ordered direct from the publisher at www.pavilionbooks.com

SIMON ARMSTRONG

COOL ArchiTecture

Filled with faNTaSTic Facts for KiDs of aLL Ages

Contents

Welcome to *Cool Architecture*

Imagine you are awake in a dream. Now, imagine you are standing in a field all by yourself and it is your job to make sense of all the space that surrounds you. Imagine that you could build a house, a fortress, or any piece of architecture that you wanted. It could be big, small, HUGE, any colour you want, any shape you want, and made out of any material you wanted. You wouldn't have to lift anything – your mind would do it all for you.

What would you design in your mind? How would you build it... and for what purpose? These are the conundrums faced by all architects since humankind first made shelters in caves, from the early Egyptians right up to the people who designed the building you are sitting in right now. Architecture has been one of the pivotal constants in human evolution; it comes in all shapes and sizes, for all purposes and intentions. Don't be ashamed to say it – Architecture is cool.

Every building in the world is built for a reason. Some are meant to be lived in, others are for businesses, schools, palaces or sport. When you start to look closely at buildings – the people who built or lived in them, how they were built, and what they were used for – you can learn a lot about history but also have grand designs on how the future may look too.

The book you are now holding is a magic key to the lock of an enormous castle called Architecture. Open it up and explore the incredible feats of engineering, ingenious inventions and the outer limits of human architectural achievement, from the minute to the massive.

Our goal for this book is to help you see the constructed environment around you with a clearer, keener eye, and perhaps inspire you to start designing and building skyscrapers yourself! The world will always need architects, just like it will always need shelter and spaces for people to live, work and play in.

Enjoy the book – now wake up, and start creating your very own castles in the sky!

'Every great architect is – necessarily – a great poet. He must be a great original interpreter of his time, his day, his age.'

Frank Lloyd Wright

Cool Timeline: Architecture Through History

Architecture comes in all shapes and sizes, forms and themes, and has existed for many thousands of years, since humankind first realised it was much nicer to sleep in a dry cave than in a muddy puddle. Here are the main themes throughout history, so you can build a picture in your mind of how they inspire and influence and contrast with each other...

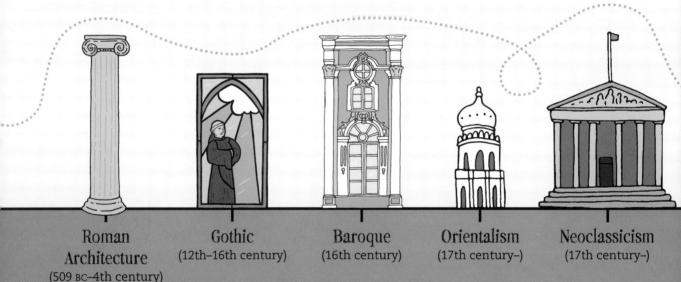

Roman Architecture
(509 BC–4th century)

Gothic
(12th–16th century)

Baroque
(16th century)

Orientalism
(17th century–)

Neoclassicism
(17th century–)

THE BLUEPRINT

Over the centuries building materials have evolved from twigs, ice, mud, clay, sand, stone, thatch and timber to cement, concrete, fabric, foam, glass, gypcrete, metal and plastics. What will the future be made of?

THINK OUTSIDE THE BOX

The word Architecture comes from the Greek word *arkhitekton*, meaning 'chief builder'.

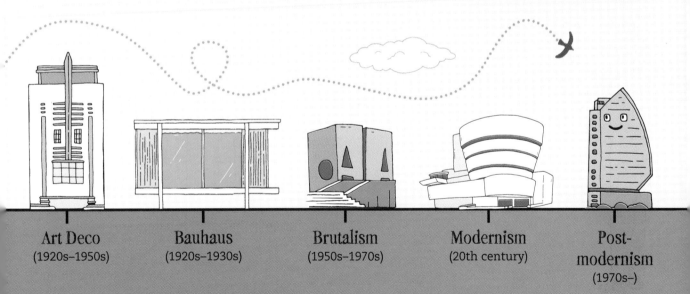

Art Deco
(1920s–1950s)

Bauhaus
(1920s–1930s)

Brutalism
(1950s–1970s)

Modernism
(20th century)

Post-modernism
(1970s–)

How to Draw Like an Architect

Before you can start building, you need to get your ideas down on paper. Drawing sketches and plans that are easy for builders to understand is essential. You don't want the building falling down now, do you? Over the centuries, architects have developed a particular style of drawing to express their ideas. Here's how you can do it too.

Building Blocks

A line drawn by an architect can be instantly recognised by the emphasis at the beginning and the end of each stroke. It's a deliberate style that pins a line to a page and looks confident and strong.

1. Train yourself to draw strong lines by pressing your pen down on the page for a moment before you start to draw the line and again when you reach the end.

2. Ensure that each whole line is drawn in a single, controlled stroke. Never make a line out of several short ones joined together.

3. You could draw a faint line first, before drawing the final solid line on top. It's okay to leave these light guidelines on the page afterwards because they add character to the sketch, so there's no need to erase them.

What is a blueprint?

In the 19th century architects started to use light-sensitive paper that enabled them to make many copies of a drawing very quickly and then give identical copies out to engineers and builders. The sheets were blue and the lines white, a 'negative' of the original. The method was used well into the 20th century but is now obsolete, although the term 'blueprint' is often still used by architects when talking about a design or building plan.

THE BLUEPRINT

Before you begin sketching, pick up these essential architectural tools:

- A fineliner pen
- A mechanical pencil
- Coloured pencils
- A pencil sharpener: all pencils need to be very sharp at all times!
- A set square
- A rolling parallel rule
- A scale rule
- A circle template
- An eraser

4. When a line meets another, overlap them. This improves the solidity and sharpness of the sketch and stops corners looking loose or rounded.

5. Draw omnipotently! Never complete the drawing of one area in full detail before moving onto the next. Keep the whole project in view by sketching the complete picture out first and gradually filling in detail across the whole page, completing the full drawing at the same time.

The Great Pyramids of Giza

Imhotep, the great Egyptian polymath often regarded as the world's first architect, was a god. He designed the most wonderful of all the wonders of the world: the Great Pyramids of Giza.

Building Blocks

The Egyptians set the standard for what most people recognise as classic pyramid design: massive monuments with a square base and four smooth-sided

triangular sides, rising to a point. One of the most famous earliest pieces of architecture still standing is the Great Pyramids of Giza. They are perhaps the most defining, and first, architectural wonder of the world!

Khufu =
146.5m
(481ft)
high

Another Level

The three pyramids that were built together over 4500 years ago near Giza in Egypt are called Khufu, Khafre and Menkaure and are named after the rulers buried inside each one. Hundreds of thousands of workmen lifted stones into place using a system of ropes and pulleys. Each pyramid took around 25 years to complete.

Khufu is the Great Pyramid, standing at 146.5m (481ft) high. It is surrounded by several smaller pyramids for Pharaoh Khufu's family. Near the Great Pyramid is the huge Sphinx, a statue of the Pharaoh's head on a lion's body.

Take it to the Top!

Each pyramid is built on a perfectly square base. Each triangular side is aligned with the compass points North, South, East and West. It remains a mystery, even to architects in the

THE BLUEPRINT

Built 2500 BC (over 4500 years ago!)

The Pyramids of Giza are the oldest of the Seven Wonders of the World and the only ones that still exist. Each pyramid was originally covered with smooth white stone, which would have made them shine like gold in the Egyptian sun. These white stones were removed and used for other buildings around the 14th century.

twenty-first century, how they were built with such precision with such limited technology.

The large stones that make up the Great Pyramid each weigh 2250kg (4960lb – the weight of four camels!) and are thought to have been transported from over 800km (500 miles) away. Moving just one of these blocks that distance without any machinery would have been extremely difficult, but the Great Pyramid is built with 2.3 million of them!

The Egyptians must have known a great deal about construction, mathematics and science in order to build the pyramids. That they are still standing today is a tribute to their genius!

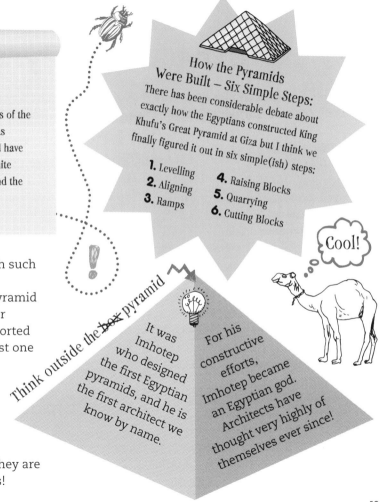

How the Pyramids
Were Built – Six Simple Steps:
There has been considerable debate about exactly how the Egyptians constructed King Khufu's Great Pyramid at Giza but I think we finally figured it out in six simple(ish) steps:

1. Levelling
2. Aligning
3. Ramps
4. Raising Blocks
5. Quarrying
6. Cutting Blocks

Cool!

Think outside the ~~box~~ pyramid

It was Imhotep who designed the first Egyptian pyramids, and he is the first architect we know by name.

For his constructive efforts, Imhotep became an Egyptian god. Architects have thought very highly of themselves ever since!

The Vitruvian Man

Imhotep may have been the first known architect of the world, but it was his Roman heir (in spirit, at least) Marcus Vitruvius Pollio who, quite literally, wrote the modern rulebook for architecture.

Building Blocks

Vitruvius' *De Architectura*, believed to have been written around 15 BC, is the only text on the subject of architecture that survived from the days of Ancient Rome. It was also one of the first texts ever to describe a connection between the human body's own architecture and that of a constructed building. According to Vitruvius, an architect's designs must relate to his body's own symmetry and sense of proportions. Vitruvius summarised that if a building is to create a sense of *'eurythmia'* – a beautiful atmosphere – it must mirror the laws of nature.

Another Level

Vitruvius believed that every architect should only focus on three central themes when designing a building:

1

FIRMITAS
(strength: a building should be able to stand up!)

2

UTILITAS
(functionality: it should also be suitable for the purposes for which is it used.)

3

VENUSTAS
(beauty: it should look lovely too!)

When it came to original thinking the Romans had it nailed. These ingenious Italians invented many of the world's first, and favourite, innovations that quite literally paved the way for the inception of the modern world. These are the architectural inventions the Ancient Romans are most remembered for:

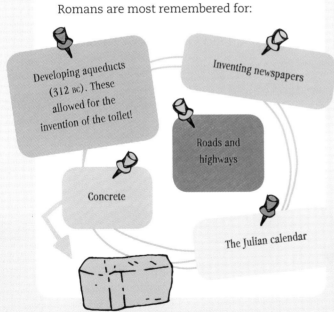

Developing aqueducts (312 BC). These allowed for the invention of the toilet!

Inventing newspapers

Roads and highways

Concrete

The Julian calendar

THE BLUEPRINT

The Vitruvian Man

Leonardo da Vinci – you know the one! – produced a drawing in 1490 of human scale called 'The Vitruvian Man'. Based on Vitruvius' ideas, da Vinci identified aspects of proportion and scale and that each separate part of a body was a simple fraction of the whole. For example, the head measured from the forehead to the chin is always exactly one tenth of a person's total height, and that when a person's arms are outstretched they are always as wide as the body is tall. Da Vinci's famous quote is, 'Man is the model of the world,' – and he believed that everything in the world should be centred around the human body.

Going Up in the World: Columns!

If you want a building to stand up, you'll need some sort of support. Ladies and gentlemen, the number one magic ingredient of architecture is, of course, columns...

Building Blocks

Columns are essential to every architect. Without columns, buildings would not be able to support additional levels or a roof. But there is more to columns than meets the eye...

A column is any vertical support structure, and can be seen in every kind of building. Columns became a fundamental part of architecture in 600 BC when the Ancient Greek architects developed their designs for public buildings. Modern skyscrapers are built on a frame of vertical columns and horizontal beams.

Another Level

The Greeks devised three types of column, which became known as 'orders'. The orders went on to have a huge influence in Ancient Greece and Rome, and then much later in Europe and America, making the orders one of the most important ideas in the history of architecture.

THINK OUTSIDE THE BOX

It's possible that the Ancient Greek stonemasons were influenced by the Egyptians. The shrine of Anubis at the Temple of Hatshepsut in Egypt has columns which closely resemble Doric columns!

THE BLUEPRINT

The post-and-lintel system is a system in which two upright columns hold up a third column, the lintel, laid horizontally across their top surfaces. All doors and entrances to buildings have evolved from this system, developed by the Romans.

This is a column. The feature that crowns the top of a column is called a capital.

There are three column types:

DORIC
has a plain capital.

IONIC
has a capital that looks like a scroll.

CORINTHIAN
has capitals decorated with leaves of the acanthus plant.

The Doric order was first used around 590 BC, followed by the Ionic and then the Corinthian. Doric columns are said to represent the beauty of masculinity, while Ionic columns, more delicate and adorned, celebrate the female form. The Corinthian columns, being slender and decorated with leaves, are said to represent young maidens.

Take it to the Top!
The Romans came along much later (around 15 AD) and added two further orders; the Tuscan, which is a very plain type of column, and the Composite, which is a highly ornate combination of both the Ionic scrolls and the acanthus leaves of the Corinthian.

Plan, Section and Elevation

Now we've learned how to draw, we can start planning our building. We're on the way to becoming an architect, but first, we must learn about Plans, Sections and Elevations...

Plan

A floor plan, or layout, of a building provides a map of the building's area and all its surrounding spaces, interior and exterior. The plan is the first thing an architect must complete, and no other stage of design or construction can go ahead without it. Why not create your own plan? Start with your own house – map out every room and space, for every level, on a piece of paper.

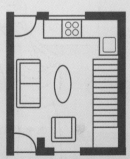

Ground Floor

Section

The section is a complementary drawing to the plan – a drawing made by cutting an imaginary vertical slice through a building, showing the ceiling heights of each floor. Together they convey essential information about the interior of a building.

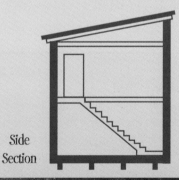

Side Section

Elevation

A drawing of one side of the exterior of a building, such as the façade or entrance. All construction plans are made up of a combination of plans, sections and elevations. Now the construction plan is complete and we are ready to build!

Front Elevation

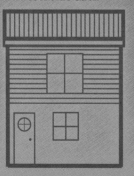

THINK OUTSIDE THE BOX

Sarah Pardee Winchester was the heir to the Winchester rifle fortune – but her inheritance came with a curse. After her husband died, she became haunted by the ghosts of anyone who had been killed by a Winchester rifle – potentially more than a million ghosts! Determined to rid herself of the curse, Mrs. Winchester started building a grand house to appease the spirit world, with one goal: to never, ever, finish building it. To be successful, the construction would need to be carried out 24 hours a day, seven days a week! Mrs Winchester bought the now-famous Winchester Mystery House in San Jose, California, a historical landmark. From the outside, the 160-room house looks beautiful. But the inside paints the picture of a lonely, scared woman slowly losing her mind. Room after room, staircase after staircase, was built on a whim over the span of 38 years. There was no floor plan – she just kept building. Some doors lead straight into brick walls. One doorway on the second floor leads outside to *absolutely* nothing – no staircase, no balcony, no hallway. If you were to walk out this door you'd fall two storeys! More than 2000 windows were built facing walls, offering no view. Multiple rooms in the house also have 13 windows. It is an architectural oddity that has to be seen to be believed!

Here Come the Romans!

What have the Romans ever done for architecture? Quite a lot it seems! The Roman Empire lasted from 509 BC to 476 AD, and when they weren't busy conquering other nations, they were living the high life, surrounding themselves with beauty, including their buildings!

Building Blocks

Emperor Augustus (63 BC–14 AD) ordered that Rome was to be made beautiful, and a city-wide building project using influences taken from the ancient Greeks was immediately put into action. Roman inventions, such as bath-houses, underfloor heating and plumbing, greatly improved the function of architecture of the time, developed using Greek methods. Roman architects used columns and sculptures to adorn buildings.

Another Level

One major architectural leap forward by the Romans was the invention of concrete – a mixture of sand, water and gravel. Using concrete, Roman architects discovered they could build thick, solid walls very quickly. Concrete was also perfect for smooth curved surfaces such as the vaulted ceilings and domes that can be seen on the Pantheon.

THINK OUTSIDE THE BOX

Pozzolana is a mixture of lime and volcanic ash that the Romans discovered around the Bay of Naples and used to bind concrete. This made Roman concrete so strong that 2000 years after they were built, when all the other masonry had been stolen or washed away by rain, the concrete walls still stand.

THE BLUEPRINT

The world's most famous examples of Roman architecture are still available to visit in all their original splendour and include the Pont du Gard aqueduct, Nimes, France (built 15 AD), the Temple of Venus, Rome (135 AD) and the Baths of Diocletian, Rome (306 AD). Go see them for yourself and get inspired!

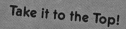

Take it to the Top!

Around 70 AD, Roman Emperor Vespasian demanded that the largest amphitheatre in the world be built in Rome. This enormous stadium was designed to host the most popular sport in the Roman era: gladiator fights. Today, the building is known as the Colosseum.

The Colosseum

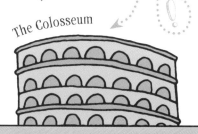

The Great Age of Castles

Castles. They are the stuff of fairytales for most of us, but for architects they were the first step towards fusing beauty with purpose. Over the centuries, castles have accommodated and protected kings and queens from invaders. Now, mostly, they are tourist hotspots!

Building Blocks

Across Europe, around 400 AD, villages were constantly at war and invading each other to plunder food, animals and land. It was a lawless time and a dangerous one in which to live. The smart thing to do was to move your settlement to the top of a hill, and build a defensive structure around it. At first, these were wooden structures, forts, but over time, after many of these structures had been burnt down by enemies, stone became the material of choice. It was now the age of the castle...

When it comes to building castles, you'll need loads of mortar. This is a paste used to bind building blocks such as stones, bricks, and concrete together, fill and seal the gaps between them, and sometimes add decorative colours or patterns on the walls.

Another Level

As Europe became ruled by law, living in castles was not quite as necessary, and people began to live in towns and cities instead. Many castles fell out of use and were dismantled or became ruins. Others were adapted into homes for the powerful and rich, which saw castles transformed into luxury palaces!

How to Build Your Own Castle
Castles are expensive (only build one if you really need one).

You'll need around 3000 workers, including masons, quarrymen, blacksmiths and carpenters.

Castles take about 10 years to build, depending on size.

Rent some horse-drawn wagons to haul the stone you're going to use from the quarry to the building site.

The masons on the wall fit the stones together and use the mortar to hold the blocks together.

Make mortar on the site from lime, soil and water.

Craftsmen use a long rope with knots placed every metre to measure wooden beams and lay out pieces.

They then use a wooden triangle with a line and plumb bob suspended from one angle as a level when placing stones.

Now build upwards!

THINK OUTSIDE THE BOX

The most popular – and some say, most beautiful – castle in the world is Mont Saint-Michel in France, located on a rocky tidal island in Normandy, 1km (half a mile) offshore. The island's highest point is 92m (301ft) above sea level, protecting it from scallywags intent on storming it! It is now a UNESCO World Heritage Site and visited by more than three million people each year. The strong tides in the area change quickly, so if you visit, make sure you don't get stuck there!

Material World

We all live in a material world. Without the right tools and materials architects would never be able to leave their drawing boards. Let's construct a building, and toast to the four magic materials used in architecture...

Building Blocks

In architecture's history there are trends in building materials. From natural (wood, ice) to becoming more man-made and composite (plastics); biodegradable to imperishable; indigenous (local) to being transported globally; repairable to disposable.

① Wood
An ideal building material, wood is lightweight but also very strong and durable. The two classifications are hardwood and softwood. Hardwood is derived from deciduous trees such as oak and walnut. Softwood is from coniferous trees such as pine. Because wood can be carved and shaped, it's quite easy to join pieces together.

② Masonry
The basic principles of masonry building are exactly the same as they were in ancient times. Bricks, stone and concrete come from the earth, and are suitable as foundations and walls. Their strength and durability makes them much more resistant to the elements of fire, water and wind than wood.

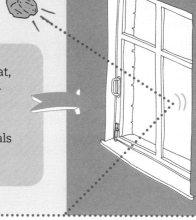

THINK OUTSIDE THE BOX

There are now all kinds of glass available: some resist heat, or bullets, or change colour at different times of day. Self-cleaning glass has a special coating that breaks down dirt, photovoltaic glass has solar cells embedded in it to convert solar energy into electricity and x-ray protection glass is used in hospitals to reduce exposure to radiation.

3 Metal

Metal features in almost every part of a building project, from structural frames to heating pipes, down to the humble nails pinning everything together. Even the paint for the walls is full of metal oxides for pigmentation. Metal is mined and then refined to separate it from other elements and impurities. The two categories are ferrous (containing iron) and nonferrous. Ferrous metals are usually stronger, but can also rust. Nonferrous metals are much easier to work with and less likely to corrode.

4 Glass

Glass is made using a carefully measured-out recipe of soda, silica sand, calcium oxide and magnesium. All the ingredients go into a furnace at 1500 degrees Celsius, where they melt over a bath of molten tin. The mixture is then slowly cooled and flattened into panes for windows! Glass was first discovered in Roman times, but wasn't used again until the Middle Ages, then became commonplace from the 18th century.

Divine Inspiration

Some of the world's earliest, and greatest, pieces of architecture were originally created for places of worship and took the form of churches, mosques, synagogues and temples. Without religion – and building landmarks designed to impress gods and pray to them – architecture may not have taken as many brave leaps forward as it did...

Building Blocks
Sacred architecture and places of worship make up some of the most impressive man-made buildings. Until skyscrapers were built in the 20th century (and almost so high they tickle God's bottom!), religious landmarks and places of worship were the largest structures ever built.

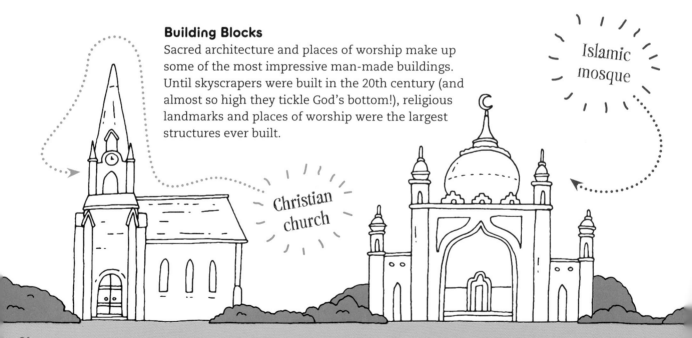

Islamic mosque

Christian church

Another Level

The history of architecture, in general, runs parallel to the history of religious architecture, up until the Baroque period, when non-secular buildings began to take a more central role.

Much of the design, geometry and use of motifs and symbols in architecture are born out of sacred landmarks.

THINK OUTSIDE THE BOX

Church towers are often topped with a tall, pointed extension known as a spire or steeple. They were popular from the 12th century onwards, and a variety of styles can be found through the Gothic, Baroque and Neoclassical periods up to today.

THE BLUEPRINT

The world is action-packed with religious and architectural landmarks. These are considered the greatest architecturally – and are stunning to take a look at! See for yourself:

- The Pantheon, Rome
- Temple Complex of Karnak, Thebes, Egypt
- The Temple Mount, Jerusalem
- The Temple of the Jaguar, Tikal, Guatemala
- Angkor Wat, Cambodia
- The Meteora Monasteries, Greece
- The Ziggurat of Ur, Iraq
- Pyramids of Teotihuacan, Mexico
- Delphi, Greece
- Borobudur, Indonesia

Hindu temple

Filippo Brunelleschi

A painter, sculptor and skilled goldsmith from Florence, Italy, Filippo Brunelleschi became one of the great architects of the early Renaissance (14th–17th century), most noted for the domed cathedral in Florence and his invention of linear perspective in art and architecture.

Building Blocks

Brunelleschi was commissioned by the wealthiest and most powerful family in Florence, the Medicis, to build a chapel (The Old Sacristy) in the Florentine church of San Lorenzo. He did such an impressive job, the Medicis immediately entrusted him to rebuild the entire church!

Another Level

However, the workers employed to build the enormous new dome for the Florence Cathedral were doubtful. The diameter was 45m (147ft); everyone thought it was impossible to build a dome so large without it collapsing. But Brunelleschi had a plan: he would build two domes, one inside the other. The inner one would be the strong, load-bearing dome that would then support the larger, outer dome. Problem solved!

'No other memory remains of us than the walls, which after hundreds and thousands of years still bear witness to him who was their author.'
Vasari, writing about Brunelleschi

Take it to the Top!

Brunelleschi was inventive in other ways too. As the dome was being built, he installed a temporary wine bar and kitchen in the roof of the cathedral, so the workers could have a lunch-break without climbing all the way down to the ground and back up again. They were happier, and worked faster!

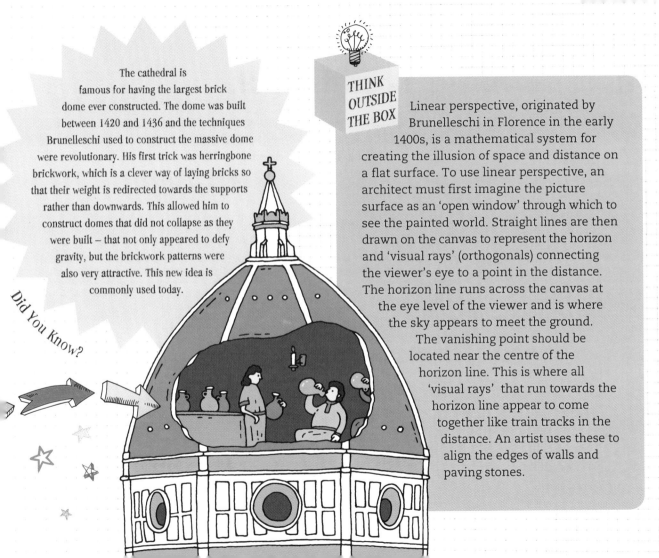

The cathedral is famous for having the largest brick dome ever constructed. The dome was built between 1420 and 1436 and the techniques Brunelleschi used to construct the massive dome were revolutionary. His first trick was herringbone brickwork, which is a clever way of laying bricks so that their weight is redirected towards the supports rather than downwards. This allowed him to construct domes that did not collapse as they were built – that not only appeared to defy gravity, but the brickwork patterns were also very attractive. This new idea is commonly used today.

Did You Know?

THINK OUTSIDE THE BOX

Linear perspective, originated by Brunelleschi in Florence in the early 1400s, is a mathematical system for creating the illusion of space and distance on a flat surface. To use linear perspective, an architect must first imagine the picture surface as an 'open window' through which to see the painted world. Straight lines are then drawn on the canvas to represent the horizon and 'visual rays' (orthogonals) connecting the viewer's eye to a point in the distance. The horizon line runs across the canvas at the eye level of the viewer and is where the sky appears to meet the ground. The vanishing point should be located near the centre of the horizon line. This is where all 'visual rays' that run towards the horizon line appear to come together like train tracks in the distance. An artist uses these to align the edges of walls and paving stones.

Building With Light!

Gothic architecture arose in Northern Europe during the Middle Ages. During this period, the Church dominated all aspects of culture, so it's no surprise that the best examples of Gothic are cathedrals and monasteries. Gothic is all about height, light and extraordinary geometry!

Building Blocks

In the 12th century a monk by the name of Suger was elected to run the monastery of St Denis in France. Suger believed that the greatest expression of God was through light, so he set about rebuilding his church in 1122, filling it with bright colours and polished metal. He positioned large stained glass windows on all sides, casting aside the gloomy, solemn style of earlier churches. He had created the first Gothic church!

Another Level

Pointed arches, stone vaults and flying buttresses were all constructed to dramatically raise the height of the ceiling, giving the impression that the building was reaching up to Heaven. The effect this had on the people in the church was to make them feel humble, and wonder at the enormity of God and the heavens. The style was so effective that it was copied throughout Europe. Gothic construction styles soon became the dominant western architecture for the next 300 years.

The Gothic style of architecture features three consistent elements:

① ROSE WINDOWS

Twelve glass petals radiate outwards to form the centre of the window. Twelve is a 'divine' number, associated with the signs of the zodiac and the disciples.

② ORNAMENTATION

Carvings of saints, animals and gargoyles decorated cathedral walls. The gargoyles had a dual purpose; rainwater would run into them and out of their mouths, stopping the walls and entrances from becoming damp, but they were also placed there to stop the devil from entering the building!

③ TELLING THE STORY OF THE BIBLE

The building itself would often be designed and decorated to relate biblical tales. The stained glass windows told pictorial stories from the Bible, and carvings (called reliefs) of the saints were set into archways.

THINK OUTSIDE THE BOX

One of the most famous examples of Gothic architecture is The Church of Our Lady of Ingolstadt in Bavaria. Here are some other classic examples:

- Cologne Cathedral, Cologne, Germany
- Milan Cathedral, Milan, Italy
- Notre Dame de Paris, Paris, France
- Canterbury Cathedral, Canterbury, Kent, UK
- Saint Vitus Cathedral, Prague, Czech Republic

Life's Better With Bridges

Without bridges, humans would be metaphorically, and literally, stuck. There is no greater symbol of the skill and effort we use to make progress than the bridge; an often humble but essential architectural feature that enables business and travel and connects millions of people together.

Building Blocks
There are four main types of bridges:

1. Beam Bridge
This type of bridge is the easiest to build. It is a single deck supported on each side. Beam bridges work best when they are short; the longer they are the more likely they are to bend in the middle. If the bridge needs to be longer, it's best to make a truss bridge. A beam bridge can be as simple as a tree trunk or plank of wood across a gap.

2. Truss Bridge
To cover a distance, and to be affordable, a beam bridge can be strengthened using a framework of lightweight triangles. The framework is stronger than a simple beam, the weight evenly distributed. Think of a cobweb, which needs to be very strong but very lightweight at the same time.

What allows an arch bridge to span greater distances than a beam bridge, or a suspension bridge to stretch over a distance seven times that of an arch bridge? The answer lies in how each bridge type deals with the important forces of compression and tension. Compression and tension are present in all bridges. It's the job of the bridge designed by the architect to handle these forces without making them bend, break or buckle in half!

How Bridges Work

Tension: Think of a game of tug-of-war. What happens to the rope? It undergoes tension from the two teams pulling on it.

Compression: Think of a spring. What happens when you push down on it? You compress it, and by squashing it, you shorten its length.

3. Arch Bridge

This kind of bridge is rather like a suspension bridge turned upside down. The deck sits on the top and is supported from below. As weight pushes down on the deck, the arch sends the pressure to each side, rather than downward, so the bridge can carry heavy loads without collapsing.

4. Suspension Bridge

This style of bridge is supported from above by long cables fastened to the top of tall vertical towers. It's a clever way to make a very long bridge. Famous examples include the Golden Gate Bridge in San Francisco and Tower Bridge, London.

Andrea Palladio

The Renaissance (meaning 'Rebirth') was the famous period around the 15th and 16th centuries when the arts and sciences flourished over religion. One of the great influences on Western architecture was Andrea Palladio, whose work embodies the style of the famous Renaissance period and was strongly based on symmetry, perspective and the values of classical Ancient Greek and Roman architecture.

Building Blocks

Andrea Palladio was born Andrea della Gondola in 1508 in Italy and was apprenticed as a stonemason aged 13. He worked as a mason and sculptor for 30 years, until he was employed by Gian Giorgio Trissino to work on a villa. While there Palladio was introduced to Renaissance culture, including the architectural ideas of Vitruvius.

Another Level

Palladio designed at least 30 villas in his lifetime, all inspired by the rural villas of ancient Rome. His most famous work is Villa Capra, known as 'La Rotonda', which influenced many later architects.

Take it to the Top!

Published in 1570, Palladio's famous essay *I Quattro Libri Dell'Architettura (The Four Books of Architecture)* is the foundation stone of modern architecture's rules and became so vital to architecture that the movement following Palladio's era is named after him – Palladian architecture. *I Quattro Libri Dell'Architettura* celebrates the simplicity of classical architecture and contains many of Palladio's own designs.

'The place is nicely situated and one of the loveliest and most charming that one could hope to find; for it lies on the slopes of a hill, which is very easy to reach. The loveliest hills are arranged around it, which afford a view into an immense theatre. Because one takes pleasure in the beautiful view on all four sides, loggias were built on all four facades.'

Palladio, on La Rotonda

THINK OUTSIDE THE BOX

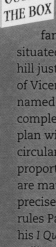

La Rotonda is Palladio's most famous work. It's situated on the top of a hill just outside the town of Vicenza, Italy, and is so named because of its completely symmetrical plan with a central circular hall. The proportions of each room are mathematically precise, according to the rules Palladio describes in his *I Quattro Libri Dell'Architettura*. The building is rotated 45 degrees to the south on the hilltop, making sure all rooms are bathed in sunshine.

COOL MOVEMENTS

Baroque and Roll

The Baroque architectural style began in 17th-century Italy. Baroque was both an extension of the Renaissance period that preceded it and also a reaction against it.

Building Blocks

Classical elements in architecture were now established and combined in ever more complex ways, giving buildings a sense of physical motion and emotional intensity.

The word 'Baroque' is from the Portuguese term to describe 'an oddly shaped pearl' but in art, architecture and design, Baroque describes anything elaborate and grand.

THINK OUTSIDE THE BOX

Rococo

A variety of Baroque that evolved in France and Germany, Rococo architecture is highly decorative, associated with S-shaped and C-shaped curves, motifs of scallop shells, fruit, flowers and scrolls and bright colours set against pale pastels. Rococo has had a big impact on architecture and also design, including furniture and ceramics.

Another Level

In practice, Baroque is, essentially, a new treatment of space. Renaissance architecture had been mainly concerned with geometry and simple shapes – cubes, triangles and domes – but Baroque added much more detail and sophistication. Domes could now be oval, lines didn't have to be straight, columns could be twisted, walls could be curved.

FAMOUS BAROQUE EXAMPLES:

Sanssouci Palace, Potsdam, Germany (1745)

Catherine Palace, Russia (rebuilt by Bartolomeo Rastrelli, 1752)

Schloss Solitude, Germany (Philippe de la Guêpière, 1764)

Take it to the Top!
The Baroque style quickly spread from Rome, through Italy and across Europe. Royalty and the Church were particular fans, leading to many new churches and palaces in this style. The grandest of them all was the Palace of Versailles near Paris built for King Louis XIV.

The Taj Mahal

In 1600, the powerful Mughal Empire ruled lands that included most of what is known today as India. The emperor, Shah Jahan, was their mighty leader. When his third (and favourite) wife Mumtaz Mahal died in 1632, while giving birth to their 14th child, he was heartbroken, and ordered that a glorious monument be built in her honour and memory.

Building Blocks

The Taj Mahal, designed by Indian architect Ahmad Lahauri, took around 20 years to construct and 22,000 workers to build. It is made entirely of white marble. It has 22 domes and four minarets, which are the tall towers around the edge of the foundations. The minarets are not straight, they lean outward, away from the main building. They were designed this way in case of earthquakes, so if they collapsed, they would fall away from the mausoleum.

Another Level

The Taj Mahal is very cool. But just how cool is it exactly?

1. The Taj Mahal's interior is decorated with 28 different types of precious gemstones.

2. The white marble used in the Taj Mahal is delicate. To protect it from air pollution, cars are not allowed within 2000m (6,500 feet) of the building.

THINK OUTSIDE THE BOX

The Taj Mahal takes on different colouring at different times of the day, from a pinkish hue in the morning to a milky white in the evening and even golden at night when lit by the moon.

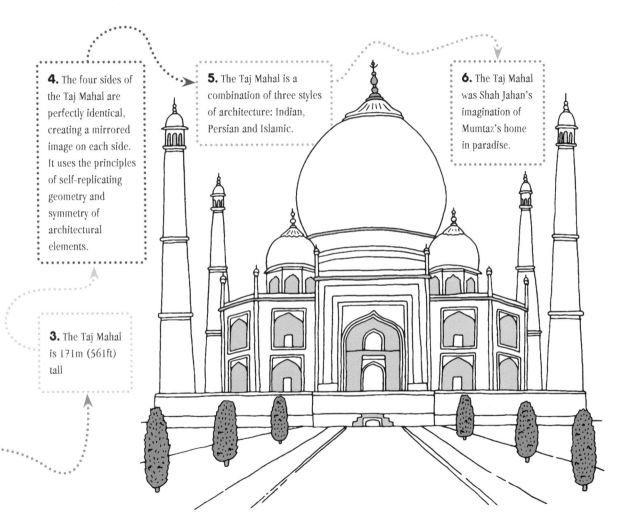

4. The four sides of the Taj Mahal are perfectly identical, creating a mirrored image on each side. It uses the principles of self-replicating geometry and symmetry of architectural elements.

5. The Taj Mahal is a combination of three styles of architecture: Indian, Persian and Islamic.

6. The Taj Mahal was Shah Jahan's imagination of Mumtaz's home in paradise.

3. The Taj Mahal is 171m (561ft) tall

Home Sweet Dome

Domes are a key innovation in architecture. First used by the Romans, they then became a key design feature of Renaissance and Neoclassical architecture.

Invented by the Inuit community, igloos have been around for centuries – the first dome ever built was perhaps an igloo by an Eskimo. One of the most recent domes constructed was the Millennium Dome, London by famed architect Richard Rogers.

Building Blocks

In Italian Renaissance architecture, the dome was a defining feature of many cathedrals, Florence Cathedral being the most dramatic. Many cathedral buildings were simply called 'Duomo'. Domes are still regularly used and constructed today, in increasingly complex ways.

Another Level

A spherical, oval or polygonal roof, such as a dome, is technically a type of vault (see page 68). It is used to define a space inside a building and also to give it a strong presence from the outside. Before domes were invented, nearly all ancient structures were supported by columns. The columns served their purpose of supporting the roof but didn't provide much interior space. Domes solved this problem as they are an extremely strong structure by nature and also create a large area of open space, great for public buildings. Domes are also strong because the pressure on top of it rolls off the sides and is evenly distributed.

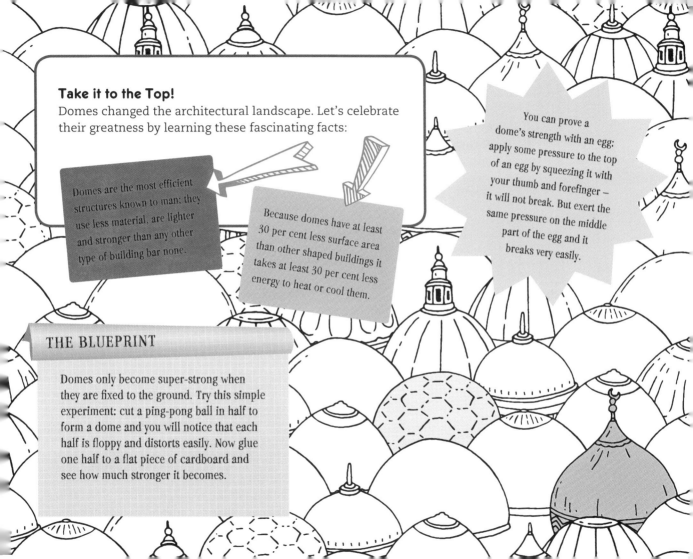

Take it to the Top!
Domes changed the architectural landscape. Let's celebrate their greatness by learning these fascinating facts:

Domes are the most efficient structures known to man: they use less material, are lighter and stronger than any other type of building bar none.

Because domes have at least 30 per cent less surface area than other shaped buildings it takes at least 30 per cent less energy to heat or cool them.

You can prove a dome's strength with an egg: apply some pressure to the top of an egg by squeezing it with your thumb and forefinger – it will not break. But exert the same pressure on the middle part of the egg and it breaks very easily.

THE BLUEPRINT

Domes only become super-strong when they are fixed to the ground. Try this simple experiment: cut a ping-pong ball in half to form a dome and you will notice that each half is floppy and distorts easily. Now glue one half to a flat piece of cardboard and see how much stronger it becomes.

Orientalism

In the late 17th century, as trade links with China and India became stronger, Europeans became fascinated with the exotic culture, customs and goods of the 'Orient'. While businessmen made their fortunes shipping tea from East to West, architecture also imported many of the motifs, styles and patterns used in Chinese and Indian buildings.

Building Blocks

Chinese pagodas, gazebos and pavilions began popping up on the estates of fashionable aristocrats all over Europe: the UK, France, Sicily and Sweden all have celebrated examples of Oriental structures.

Take it to the Top!

A British architect, Sir William Chambers, visited China several times and published a huge book in 1757 called *Designs of Chinese Buildings*, which contained engravings of many houses, bridges and temples. Most of the other architects in Britain at the time didn't take Orientalism seriously, seeing it as a passing trend. However, Chambers had friends in high places, and when the Prince of Wales, soon to be crowned King George III, commissioned him to build a Chinese pagoda in the royal gardens at Kew, the Oriental style became firmly established.

43

Theories of Architecture

There are many theories and rules when it comes to architectural design. Two of the most important are Solid-void Theory and Figure-ground Theory.

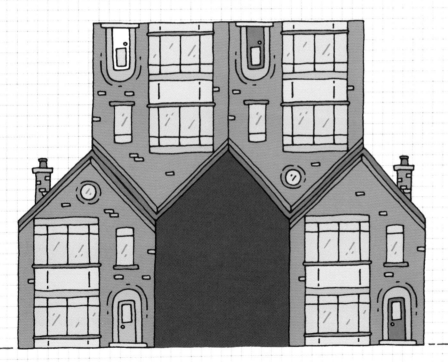

Figure-ground Theory

A 'figure' is any shape or object represented in a drawing on a page. The 'ground' is the space on the page itself. So, for example, the figure could be a house and the ground could be a field. Figure-ground theory emphasises that when designing a building, consideration should be given to the ground around a figure, rather than just the figure itself.

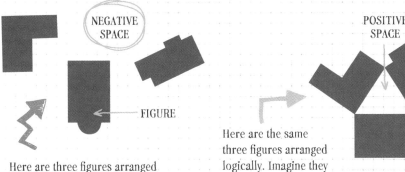

NEGATIVE SPACE

FIGURE

Here are three figures arranged without logic. The space around these is called 'negative space' because it is unstructured.

POSITIVE SPACE

Here are the same three figures arranged logically. Imagine they are three buildings. The triangular space in the middle is now a 'positive space'. Perhaps it is a garden or a courtyard.

So, now we can see how buildings can be organised, making good use of the space around them.

Solid-void Theory

Solid-void Theory follows on from the two-dimensional Figure-ground theory and applies it to the three-dimensional. Now we are dealing with the volume of space, fresh air versus solid stone. Whatever the architect builds has an impact on the open space around it.

Considerations need to be made about positive and negative space. The air around a building can 'frame' it, making it more striking. In dense cities, architects carefully plan the gaps and spaces between buildings to avoid blocking out light, cutting off views, and stopping people from feeling trapped or claustrophobic. Solid-void Theory is essential in creating a positive urban environment.

45

Sport and Architecture

Since the beginning of civilisation, people have always gathered at great stadiums to watch sport. Here are two of the great architectural sporting wonders, built 2000 years apart. Let's pit them against each other to see which one is better! Let the battle commence!

VS

THE COLOSSEUM: A Checklist – All You Need to Know

1 A stadium built over 2000 years ago for gladiator games. It was then used for 500 years as a place to watch people and animals fight each other to the death. The Colosseum could seat 50,000 people at once.

2 Over the centuries it has had a number of uses. It started out as an amphitheatre, but was later used as housing, as a fortress, as a church and even a graveyard. It is now a tourist attraction.

3 There are 80 exits around the building, to ensure the thousands of visitors could leave easily after the gladiator matches.

4 The exits were known as 'vomitoria', which is the origin of the word 'vomit', meaning fast exit! The Colosseum was designed to be vacated in under 10 minutes.

5 The building of the Ancient Roman Colosseum was politically motivated, intended for entertaining and, possibly more importantly, distracting Rome's population from more serious issues of the time such as oligarchy, nepotism and corruption in the senate and church.

BIRD'S NEST: A Checklist – All You Need to Know

1 The Bird's Nest stadium in Beijing, China, cost around 325 million euros to build.

2 The Bird's Nest architects were Herzog and de Meuron. Until they designed the Bird's Nest, Herzog and de Meuron were best known for converting London's Bankside power station into Tate Modern.

3 The number eight is believed to be very lucky in Chinese culture, so the stadium was opened on the eighth day of the eighth month of 2008, at 8.08pm!

4 The building is a concrete stadium, inside a 'nest' of steel beams, but nowhere in the building do concrete and steel touch each other.

5 The Bird's Nest architectural design is described as Expressionist Modern.

THINK OUTSIDE THE BOX

Swiss architects Herzog and de Meuron designed the Bird's Nest stadium with a revolutionary design and set standards of construction which many architects agree may not be surpassed for decades. The stadium comprises an outer skeleton of 42,000 tons of steel – three times heavier than the London 2012 stadium, and an inner 'skin' of double-layered plastic which keeps out wind and rain and filters out UVA light. The Bird's Nest is designed to last for 100 years and withstand a magnitude 8.0 earthquake!

The Three Little Pigs' Guide to Architecture

Vitruvius' first rule of architecture is that every building must be strong. A building isn't very good if it falls down, is it? Let's have a look at the world's strongest – and weakest – buildings. We'll compare notes at the end...

Building Blocks

With climate change seriously affecting the world's weather, not to mention many areas of the planet susceptible to extreme weather conditions, architects are joining forces to counter and protect buildings against the forces of nature. With advances in technology, and super-strong materials, buildings of the future will be able to stand up no matter what Mother Nature throws their way. When it comes to architecture, the stronger the better.

In the near future buildings will be made of exotic materials that we've not even seen. Right now, the world's strongest material is carbyne. This nifty nanomaterial is 200 times stronger than steel and has double the pulling strength – known as tensile strength – of graphene, another leading example of strength!

THINK OUTSIDE THE BOX

Another Level

Architects of the past were clever fellows. In China it has been revealed that the Great Wall of China – as well as many more of China's architectural wonders – remained intact for thousands of years, despite lacking the technologies of today and having to withstand devastating earthquakes. The secret is a super-strong mortar made from sticky rice! Construction workers in ancient China added sticky rice to locally sourced limestone that had been heated to a high temperature and then mixed with water. The combination of these two substances is indestructible!

Take it to the Top!

When the devastating – 9.0 on the Richter scale – earthquake of 2011 shook Japan to its core, the world watched in awe at the number of giant buildings that stood strong. It's because the Japanese are at the forefront of seismic technology.

Earthquakes shake a building in all directions – up and down, but mainly sideways. To counteract this sideways movement, the majority of Japan's buildings resist the violent shaking by swaying from side to side. One of the tallest buildings in Tokyo, the 238m (781ft) Roppongi Hills Mori Tower, swayed up to 3m (10ft) from side to side as a result of the earthquake.

THE BLUEPRINT

It made headlines around the world. In 2013, the Savar Upazila building in Dhaka, Bangladesh collapsed, killing over 1100 people. It has been described as the deadliest accidental structural failure in modern human history. The eight-storey building fell within seconds. Warnings to evacuate the building once cracks on the wall had started to appear were ignored.

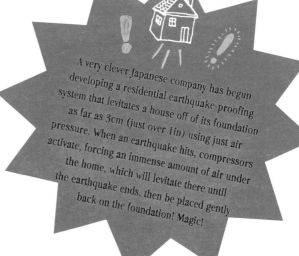

A very clever Japanese company has begun developing a residential earthquake-proofing system that levitates a house off of its foundation as far as 3cm (just over 1in) using just air pressure. When an earthquake hits, compressors activate, forcing an immense amount of air under the home, which will levitate there until the earthquake ends, then be placed gently back on the foundation! Magic!

49

Louis Sullivan

Born in 1856, Louis Sullivan, widely considered America's first truly modern architect, is remembered as the man who built Chicago, a city with almost 300 skyscrapers! A great moderniser, Sullivan rejected classical architecture and replaced the use of heavy stone with steel. With steel he was able to build the highest of high-rise skyscrapers...

In his lifetime, Sullivan's architectural firm constructed 256 projects, including the iconic Auditorium Building in Chicago. Instead of imitating historic styles, Sullivan created original forms and details. He believed that the exterior of an office building should reflect its interior structure and its interior functions. If any ornamentation was to be used it must derive from Nature, instead of from classical architecture from history.

'The Tall Office Building Artistically Considered', Louis Sullivan, 1896

'It is the pervading law of all things organic, and inorganic, of all things physical and metaphysical, of all things human and all things super-human, of all true manifestations of the head, of the heart, of the soul, that the life is recognizable in its expression, that form ever follows function. This is the law.'

Building Blocks

Sullivan coined the phrase 'Form Follows Function' to express the trend among Western architects to reject decoration. Adolf Loos also claimed that 'ornament is a crime' – everything included in a building's design has to have a useful purpose. This principle, generally now called Functionalism, goes right back to Vitruvius who claimed that a structure must have three qualities: utility, beauty and stability.

Another Level

By the early 1900s, Sullivan's work had fallen out of fashion and he faced financial ruin. At the very end of his career he designed some small commercial banks in the American Mid-West, and shortly afterwards was found dead in a cheap Chicago hotel room, alone and destitute. As tragic as his final days were, his legacy has also been laid to waste because almost all of his skyscrapers have now been demolished, but the small little banks remain.

THINK
OUTSIDE
THE BOX

The work of Louis Sullivan is often associated with the Art Nouveau movement. The best examples of Art Nouveau were made in the first decade of the 20th century. In Scotland, Charles Rennie Mackintosh built the Glasgow School of Art, Hill House, and the Willow Tea Rooms. In Barcelona, Spain, two houses by Antoni Gaudí, Casa Batlló and Casa Mila, are fine examples of the style. Over in Belgium, Victor Horta produced a number of stunning houses and hotels in the centre of Brussels.

Neoclassicism

The 18th century brought along a new generation of architects who were inspired by the antiquity styles of Greece and Rome. The early pioneering techniques were once again reappraised, revised and revived for modern appreciation...

Building Blocks

Neoclassicism arose out of a belief that the Baroque and Rococo styles of previous years had led architecture astray. Tastes had changed, and people were becoming tired of the extravagances and overblown details of Baroque and Rococo. Neoclassicism was a back-to-basics approach, inspired by two things: the intellectual climate of the Enlightenment, which valued rational thought, and an increasing number of archaeological finds, allowing architects to rediscover and reuse methods and styles from an earlier period.

THE BLUEPRINT

The emerging new discipline of Archaeology contributed to Neoclassicism. In the 1730s, archeological digs resulted in dramatic finds from Pompeii and Herculaneum. The long-buried artefacts brought people closer to history, and all things Roman and Greek became fashionable again!

Another Level

The German scholar Johann Joachim Winckelmann, inspired by his trips to Italy where he spent time admiring Roman buildings, wrote a book around 1770 showcasing the old Greek and Roman styles. The book became hugely popular and influential, making the classical style fashionable once again. Architects set about recreating the style all over Europe.

Take it to the Top!

Amazing architectural examples of Neoclassicism include:

1. Pantheon, Paris, France (Jacques-Germain Soufflot, 1796)

2. The City Theatre, Berlin (Karl Friedrich Schinkel, 1821)

3. The British Museum, London, UK (Sir Robert Smirke, 1823–46)

'We have been able to seize the beautiful spirit of antiquity, and to transfuse it with novelty and variety, through all our numerous works.'

Robert Adam

Sagrada Familia

The glorious unfinished cathedral in the centre of Barcelona, Spain, the Sagrada Familia is one of the most incredible buildings in the world.

Building Blocks

Around 1880, there was a general feeling among architects that too many buildings, particularly factories, were cold and unwelcoming. All of the new architecture was looking the same. To counteract this, many architects tried to re-connect with nature. Houses were adorned with flowers and vines and a huge variety of styles and patterns were employed to make buildings individual and homely, as if they had grown out of the ground rather than been forced upon it. The style had different names in different places, but was generally known as Art Nouveau or the Arts and Crafts Movement.

Another Level

The Spanish architect Antoni Gaudí took these ideas to an entirely new level when he started to build the church of the Sagrada Familia in Barcelona in 1883. This extraordinary building – known as the 'Cathedral of the Poor' – certainly looks like it has grown rather than been built. With towers like tall trees and pillars like branches, this beautiful, organic cathedral keeps growing!

THE BLUEPRINT

Gaudí's architecture was characterised by curves, coloured textures and shapes. Architecturally, the Sagrada Familia uses an extraordinary amount of complex features including double twisted columns, ruled surfaces, hyperboloids, hyperbolic paraboloids, helicoids and conoids and ellipsoids. They may be tongue twisters, but really these words just mean a series of shapes carved into the surface structure of the building.

'The straight line is the line of man, the curve is the line of God.'
Antoni Gaudi

Take it to the Top! Sagrada Familia Checklist:

Even after 100 years, builders and workmen are still on the site: the Sagrada Familia is still incomplete.

Construction is scheduled to finish in 2026 – the only building in the world to take 143 years to build!

It will also be one of the most expensive buildings ever made, as each year over 20 million euros are spent on the construction.

Building started in 1883, but the Sagrada Familia has only been used as a church since 2010.

The interior of the church is filled with plants carved in stone, spiral staircases and odd, angular shaped spaces. The overall effect is more like a jungle than a church!

A total of 18 spires are planned. One will be 170m (558ft) high, making it the highest spire in Europe (when they finally build it!)

Art Deco... Says Hello!

The term Art Deco started to appear after the Exposition des Arts Decoratifs in Paris in 1925, to describe any building from around the 1920s and 1930s with a sleek, modernist flair. Modernism was the dominant style at the time, which celebrated function and simplicity.

Building Blocks

If Neoclassicism was a return to the basics – where ornamentation was frowned upon – Art Deco brought decoration back, using colour and pattern and modern lines. The style draws upon classicism, and uses geometrical patterns and shapes. Motifs are inspired by Egyptian, Aztec and African art.

Another Level

What made Art Deco so appealing was that it was the first decorative style that was truly Modern. The new and luxurious style was a good match for entertainment and leisure pursuits, leading to it being adopted by many cinemas, department stores, hotels and restaurants. The two most notable Art Deco buildings in the world are found in New York: the Empire State Building and the Chrysler Building.

Take it to the Top!

The Second World War put an end to Art Deco in 1939. New buildings were put on hold during the war, and afterwards, the programme of rebuilding was done in a very sober, modern style. Art Deco came to be seen as frivolous and inappropriate after all the horrors of war.

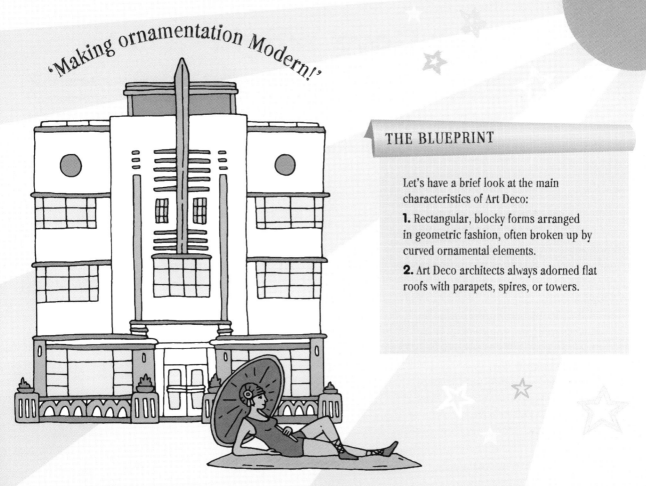

'Making ornamentation Modern!'

THE BLUEPRINT

Let's have a brief look at the main characteristics of Art Deco:

1. Rectangular, blocky forms arranged in geometric fashion, often broken up by curved ornamental elements.

2. Art Deco architects always adorned flat roofs with parapets, spires, or towers.

Frank Lloyd Wright

The prolific American architect Frank Lloyd Wright was born in 1867 and grew up on his uncle's farm in Wisconsin, USA, where he discovered the beauty of the wild countryside and nature. This influenced his later work as an architect, where he became known for creating buildings that were integrated with the climate, landscape and surrounding natural features.

Building Blocks

Lloyd Wright described his work as 'organic architecture' where 'the whole is (to) the part, what the part is to the whole.' He built many houses, but perhaps the one he is best known for is the Fallingwater house. It was a weekend retreat for Pittsburgh retailers Edgar and Liliane Kaufmann, and Lloyd Wright ensured that this home would be closely connected with nature, giving the Kaufmanns the feeling of being unified with natural surroundings.

Another Level

Fallingwater was built over a waterfall in a forest. Wright constructed stone walls built out from the rocks below, and positioned large balconies above the waterfall. Wright worked for Louis Sullivan and was hugely influenced by him, but ultimately the pair fell out when Sullivan discovered Wright was secretly working on other building designs on the side.

The house's terraces echo the pattern of the rock ledges below.

'the whole is (to) the part, what the part is to the whole.'

Wright used only four materials to build Fallingwater – sandstone, reinforced concrete, steel and glass.

Wright chose the pale ochre colour of the concrete to match the back of a fallen rhododendron leaf.

Decorating the Sky

The King of New York buildings, the Chrysler Building was built in 1928 in the heart of the city as the headquarters for one of the world's most successful car manufacturers.

Building Blocks

Architect William Van Alen was commissioned to create the tallest and most spectacular building in New York. The tower's crown is one of the world's finest examples of the Art Deco style so prevalent in the late 1920s in the USA. The entire building was designed in the style, and to remind everyone about Chrysler's motor car business, stainless steel clads the building, and car bumpers, bonnet mascots and even hubcaps are all used to decorate the tower.

319m (1046ft) tall!

Another Level

It was important to the car manufacturer's president, William P. Chrysler, that all aspects of the building and its construction demonstrated the workmanship of his company. With this in mind, the building was built extremely fast, at a rate of four floors a week!

Take it to the Top!

When the Chrysler Building's status as the tallest in New York was challenged by a new tower for the Bank of Manhattan being constructed nearby, Chrysler had a tall steel spire constructed, six storeys high, and added it to the top of the building to ensure it remained the tallest in town – and it only took 90 minutes to erect! However, it was defeated within a year by the completion of the Empire State Building, which was 381m (1250ft) high, 62m (203ft) taller than the Chrysler.

THINK OUTSIDE THE BOX The entire building contains about 400,000 rivets and over four million bricks, all laid by hand. There are also many elements of the building that reflect Chrysler's automobile empire – the famous eagle gargoyles that peek and peer on each corner of the building's roof are reminiscent of a old Chrysler hood ornament.

THE BLUEPRINT

The Chrysler Building held the title of New York's Tallest Building... for less than a year. Once the Chrysler Building was done, the Empire State architects did some figuring and decided they could make the building 85 storeys tall, eight storeys taller than the Chrysler Building. They did, of course, and the Chrysler Building was bumped to the second-tallest building in the city.

Empire State Building eight storeys taller

Ludwig Mies van der Rohe

The son of a German stone carver, Ludwig Mies left Germany for the USA when the Nazis put a stop to the production of creative art in the early 1930s. He reinvented himself by adding his mother's maiden name 'Rohe' to his own, and also the Dutch 'van der'. After many years of success in America, his career came full circle when he completed the New National Gallery in Berlin a few weeks before he died.

Building Blocks

Ludwig Mies van der Rohe first trained as a stonemason in the early 1900s, giving him a good working knowledge of building materials. He later became an architect and also the final director of the Bauhaus school of design in Germany. Just before the Second World War, he moved to the USA where he began designing houses. He was a bold architect, and his reputation was soon established through his dramatic use of metal and glass, as seen brilliantly in his other vision of the future – the Seagram Building, New York City.

Another Level

One of his most notable projects is Farnsworth House, Plano, Illinois (1951). It is a minimalist rectangular box, raised from the ground on steel posts (the area is a flood risk), with a terrace at the front. So far so good, except that every exterior wall is made from floor-to-ceiling glass. It's rather like a fish tank! This transparency makes the building unobtrusive in the landscape and allows the occupant to feel they are living in nature. Mercifully, there are curtains!

If you really want to impress your friends with your knowledge about Farnsworth House, learn these facts now!

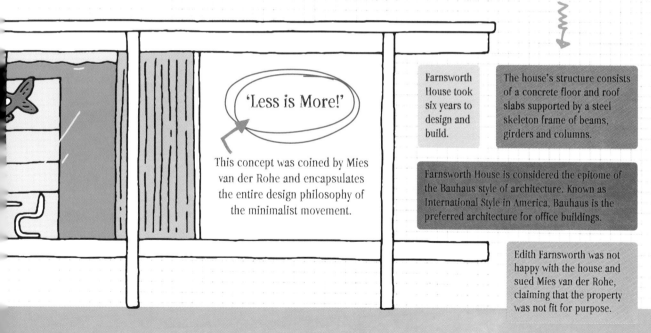

'Less is More!'

This concept was coined by Mies van der Rohe and encapsulates the entire design philosophy of the minimalist movement.

Farnsworth House took six years to design and build.

The house's structure consists of a concrete floor and roof slabs supported by a steel skeleton frame of beams, girders and columns.

Farnsworth House is considered the epitome of the Bauhaus style of architecture. Known as International Style in America, Bauhaus is the preferred architecture for office buildings.

Edith Farnsworth was not happy with the house and sued Mies van der Rohe, claiming that the property was not fit for purpose.

Ba-Ba-Ba-Ba-Bauhaus!

Bauhaus translated literally means 'house of building' which perfectly sums up the 'back to basics' approach of the architecture movement most preferred around the world for dull office buildings. But while Bauhaus meant the removal of all decoration and ornamentation, it didn't mean that buildings had to be boring...

Building Blocks

The Bauhaus school of thought sought to unite art, craft and design with the new machine age. Centred around clean geometric shapes and using only materials such as wood, metal and glass, Bauhaus design embraced a futuristic look that was also functional. This creative hub became a movement that was a source of inspiration and imitation around the world, leading the Bauhaus style to also be called 'The International Style'.

Bauhaus Checklist

What do we know about this famous architectural movement?
- Bauhaus avoids ornamentation.
- It uses asymmetry and regularity versus symmetry.
- It grasps architecture in terms of space versus mass.
- Bauhaus has a very distinct visual style: buildings are cubic, use right angles (i.e. no curves) and have smooth facades and an open floor plan.
- While one of Bauhaus' core aims was functionality, it was also among the first architectural movements to set out and prove that functional need not be boring.
  - Bauhaus buildings are usually geometric, monolithic (rectangle) skyscrapers with a flat roof and made only from stone, steel or glass materials.

Take it to the Top!

Walter Gropius designed the famous Bauhaus school building in Dessau, using large glass facades to give a sense of openness. The rest of the building was white, projecting a feeling of light. The building contained classrooms, workshops and student accommodation, and it was in this building that soon-to-become great architects such as Marcel Breuer and Mies van der Rohe worked alongside artists and artisans such as Josef Albers, Paul Klee and Wassily Kandinsky.

THINK OUTSIDE THE BOX One of the most famous examples of Bauhaus is the United Nations Secretariat, New York building designed by an international team of architects including Le Corbusier, Oscar Niemeyer, and Wallace Harrison. The smooth glass-sided slab was one of the first uses of Bauhaus' distinctive curtain-wall cladding on a tall building.

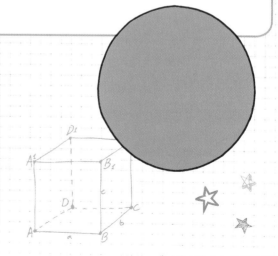

Le Corbusier's Villa Savoye

In 1929, the controversial architect Le Corbusier built Villa Savoye for the Savoy family, who allowed him free rein to apply his radical design philosophy to their home. The villa became an influential early Modernist building, admired by architects the world over.

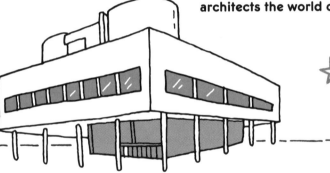

Building Blocks

Villa Savoye has a sleek industrial appearance, without ornamentation. The flat roof, open-plan interior, crisp white exterior, large horizontal ribbon windows and the stilts that raise it from the ground make this building what Le Corbusier described as 'a machine for living'.

Let's take a look at some of the characteristics of Villa Savoye

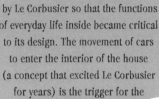
The Villa Savoye was designed by Le Corbusier so that the functions of everyday life inside became critical to its design. The movement of cars to enter the interior of the house (a concept that excited Le Corbusier for years) is the trigger for the design of the building.

Le Corbusier liked the idea that housing is designed as an object that should look like it just landed on the landscape, that is totally autonomous of its local environment and can be picked up and placed anywhere in the world.

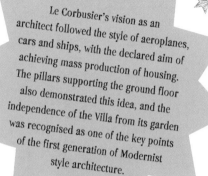
Le Corbusier's vision as an architect followed the style of aeroplanes, cars and ships, with the declared aim of achieving mass production of housing. The pillars supporting the ground floor also demonstrated this idea, and the independence of the Villa from its garden was recognised as one of the key points of the first generation of Modernist style architecture.

THE BLUEPRINT

Le Corbusier was born Charles-Edouard Jeanneret-Gris in Switzerland in 1887, but renamed himself Le Corbusier in 1920, effectively making himself a 'brand'. He was a polymath – his work combined art, writing, furniture design, town planning and of course, architecture. In 1923, Le Corbusier wrote a book called *Towards a New Architecture*. Most buildings created since then owe a debt to this 200-page guide.

TOWARDS A NEW ARCHITECTURE

Another Level

As much as Le Corbusier announced that his clinical and minimal style, which regarded furniture as 'equipment', was all about function, the Savoy family eventually found they could not live in such an austere environment. To make matters worse, the essential flat roof constantly leaked. The Savoy family moved out in 1936.

Beams, Vaults and Arches!

Architecture isn't all just about constructing cool buildings, it's also about deconstructing them and taking an in-depth look at the physical structural elements that make all themes of architecture possible.

The beam

The beam has been used since the dawn of civilisation in shelters and of course, bridges. One of the most basic structural elements required in architecture, a beam is capable of withstanding lots of weight without bending. Stone, wood and metal are the traditional materials used to construct beams, but in recent years more sophisticated, manufactured materials have become common, such as reinforced glass or 'tensioned' concrete.

The vault

A vault is a curved arched canopy above an internal space. The arched ceilings are supported by pillars and are often striking as they seem to break the laws of physics by standing so firmly. Being so strong, and fireproof, led to vaults being a commonly used innovation throughout the history of architecture. Stonemasons have developed very complicated ways of intersecting multiple vaults and joining them together.

The arch

The arch is a commonly used innovation in architecture. Quite simply, they are portals, meaning you can build a solid wall, but by adding an arch you create a way through. A bridge is the best example. You want to span a river, but you still need to let boats and water through underneath, so you build a series of arches. There are many types of arch, such as pointed Gothics and Baroque ellipticals, but while some are decoratively designed, their primary function is to create a gap to pass through while distributing weight effectively.

Architecture in the 21st Century!

Architects, and architecture, have come a long way from sketching designs and drawing up blueprints. In the modern world, building design has now moved into the digital age. Keep up!

Building Blocks

There have been four revolutions in architecture in the 21st century: Let's take a look at them:

① CAD (Computer Aided Design)
This changed everything for architects from the 1980s to today. Now all modern design and engineering is heavily reliant on CAD. Not only is planning and designing a build in 2-D and 3-D much faster and simpler with computer software, but extremely difficult calculations can be carried out in seconds, opening up a whole new world of possibility in architecture.

② Rapid Prototyping printers
These ingenious printers create three-dimensional models directly from designs made in CAD. A screw, hinge, or even a scale model of an entire building can be printed, casting aside centuries of time-consuming craft and model making.

3 Solid Modelling Software

These programs are used to produce layered 3-D images. Surfaces can be peeled off to reveal interiors of buildings – a new digital method of producing better plans and elevations without using a pencil!

4 Biomimetics

One of the most promising developments in contemporary design. With the aid of computers and science, biomimetics looks at patterns of successful evolution in nature and how organisms adapt to environments, then uses this information to make design decisions around form, structure and materials. The Al Bahr Towers in Abu Dhabi have a protective fibreglass exterior rather like fish scales. These open and close in response to the movement of the sun, reducing heat and glare.

What Goes Up... Must Come Down!

Building a structure is a lot of fun. But making a building come down again is just as much fun, too. As an architect of the future you must know how to create – and to destroy! Architecture can bring the house down – in more ways than one!

Cool!

Building Blocks

There are various reasons why buildings which took years to design, plan and construct are required to be demolished – usually in under 10 seconds! Sometimes a building just has to be knocked down to make room for another one. There are two methods for bringing down a building:

1. Deconstruction
Where a structure is slowly dismantled in pieces, usually to preserve and reuse the materials. Also known as strip-out, this process is very popular now, more so than demolition. Recycling and salvaging of materials is very attractive to builders during these austere times.

2. Demolition
Used when the building materials have no future use, so the whole building can be destroyed.

BOOM!

Another Level

In order to know about demolition we must learn about implosion. Implosion is a bursting and collapsing inward that allows the sequential elimination of structure supports. Enough explosives are used to eliminate the critical vertical structural supports. The placement of the charges and the sequential detonation timing is of vital importance, allowing the collapse of the building to be induced by the weight of the structure. Implosion demolition methods are used in urban areas and often involve large structures.

Goodbye world!

THINK OUTSIDE THE BOX
The largest ever demolition – so far – was the Sears Merchandise Center in Philadelphia, USA. This mega-structure was built by an army of 2000 workers in 1918. For 70 years it stood proud – until 5443 kilograms (12000lb) of explosives took it down in 12 seconds in 1994!

THE BLUEPRINT

With the wrecking ball now outlawed in urban demolition, architects and blast-controlling companies have had to figure out safer ways to demolish a building. The future of demolition was first demonstrated in 2008 by Kajima, a Japanese construction company, when it took down a 20-storey building from the bottom up! To do this, the company developed a system which holds up a building's support columns with giant hydraulic jacks. Deconstruction workers then cut out slices of the building at street level. Once a level has been cut away the building is lowered and the process repeated. It's like Jenga!

Architecture Down Under

One of Australia's most famous buildings – and one of the most beloved pieces of architecture on the planet – the Sydney Opera House defies all logic and belief.

Building Blocks

Danish architect Jorn Utzon became famous for building the Opera House, but not as famous as Sydney itself. It is impossible to imagine Sydney without its glorious Opera House on the harbour, a building that looks like a futuristic sailboat or a row of segments from a peeled orange.

Queen Elizabeth II opened the building in 1973, but Utzon wasn't invited to the ceremony.

The roof is made of 2194 pre-cast concrete sections.

THE BLUEPRINT

The Opera House's architectural style is described as Expressionist Modernism. This means that it involves innovative exterior shapes and the use of original materials.

THINK OUTSIDE THE BOX

The building was listed as a UNESCO World Heritage site in 2007, and is described as 'great urban sculpture set in a remarkable waterscape, at the tip of a peninsula projecting into Sydney Harbour.'

15,500 lightbulbs are changed every year at the Opera House.

There are a total of 1000 rooms in the whole building!

Another Level

Let's tick off what we know about Australia's most beautiful building:

Construction began in 1959, but the roof structure was so complicated the design had to be recalculated several times without the benefit of Computer Aided Design. This meant the building wasn't complete until 1973.

The Opera House is a huge arts centre, hosting not only opera, but also ballet, concerts and theatre. The halls inside have walls and ceilings that are carefully panelled with overlapping plywood so the music sounds perfectly clear wherever you are in the room.

Delays were caused by Utzon changing his designs as he went along. The government became very frustrated with the time and expense of the project, so started to make firmer demands and cut budgets. As his ultimate vision for the building became impossible, Utzon quit the project and left.

The roof is covered with more than one million tiles.

Utzon died at the age of 90 in 2008. He had never visited the completed Opera House.

The building is 185m (607ft) long and 120m (394ft) wide. The highest roof point is 67m (220ft) above sea level – the same as a 22-storey high building.

75

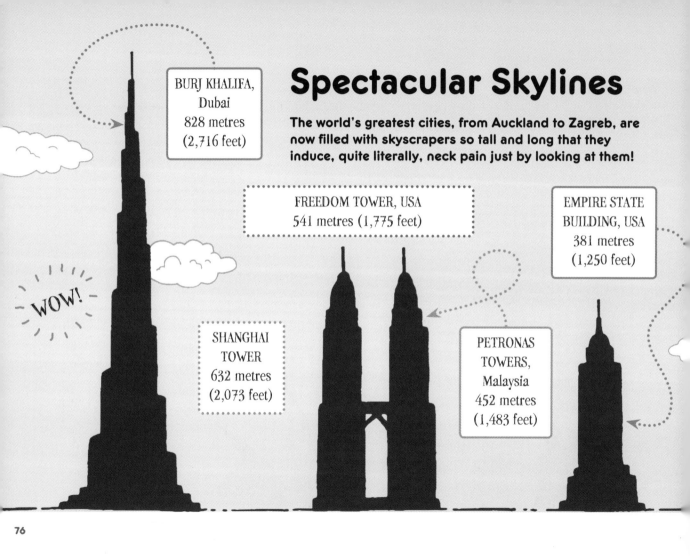

Spectacular Skylines

The world's greatest cities, from Auckland to Zagreb, are now filled with skyscrapers so tall and long that they induce, quite literally, neck pain just by looking at them!

BURJ KHALIFA, Dubai
828 metres
(2,716 feet)

FREEDOM TOWER, USA
541 metres (1,775 feet)

EMPIRE STATE BUILDING, USA
381 metres
(1,250 feet)

WOW!

SHANGHAI TOWER
632 metres
(2,073 feet)

PETRONAS TOWERS, Malaysia
452 metres
(1,483 feet)

The Freedom Tower in New York is currently being built in honour of the tragic events of September 11 2001, which witnessed large scale loss of life and the destruction of the World Trade Center Twin Towers, following attacks by the Al-Qaeda terrorist organisation. At 415m (1,362ft), One World Trade Center, as it is officially known, will have 104 floors and be a defining symbol of America's strength and honour and a proud global icon of how good always conquers evil and that no matter how many times you fall down, you must always get back up again. It is also New York's tallest skyscraper.

EIFFEL TOWER, France
324 metres
(1,063 feet)

LONDON BRIDGE TOWER
(The Shard), UK
309 metres (1,014 feet)

BIG BEN, UK
98 metres
(321 feet)

LEANING TOWER OF PISA , Italy
54 metres
(177 feet)

PERSON average height,
1.7 metres
(5ft 7in)

CCTV HEADQUARTERS, China
234 metres (768 feet)

Richard Rogers

From the Millennium Dome to the Georges Pompidou Centre, Richard Rogers is renowned for creating controversial architectural wonders as well as some of the most important buildings of the modern era. Whether you gasp or grin at his work, one thing is for sure: he will blow your socks off!

The Georges Pompidou Centre is famous not only for its fascinating exterior but also because the style of the architecture on display helped revolutionise museums. With Rogers' help, museums were no longer just for the posh members of society, but were now popular places to hang out and socialise in.

THINK OUTSIDE THE BOX

Building Blocks

Richard Rogers is an architect respected for his Modernist and functionalist designs in high-tech architecture. Also known as Late Modernism or Structural Expressionism, high-tech architecture is a style that emerged in the 1970s, and incorporated elements of high-tech industry and technology into building design. High-tech architecture appeared all over the world as a modified version of Modernism, an architectural movement that pushed the envelope of architecture even further, in part helped by sophisticated technological advances.

Take it to the Top!

As his career in architecture has progressed, Richard Rogers has increasingly turned his attention to sustainability and social justice. He understands that the architect's task is in service to people and the environment, rather than just building things. This can be seen in his 1998 building for the Welsh Assembly and his controversial housing project for the global elite: One Hyde Park. All of these projects have remarkably low energy use, with Rogers ensuring that materials and conservation are at the forefront of all his design decisions.

Awarded the Pritzker Prize in 2007

Another Level

Rogers is famous for designing several award-winning architectural wonders. Here are his greatest achievements to date:

1 CENTRE POMPIDOU, Paris, France (with Renzo Piano)

2 LLOYD'S HEADQUARTERS, London, UK

3 MILLENNIUM DOME, London, UK

4 BARAJAS INTERNATIONAL AIRPORT, Madrid, Spain

Brutalism and Beyond

The world of architecture has changed remarkably since the Romans first discovered concrete. But concrete was to come back into fashion with a bang in the 1950s – with Brutalism.

Building Blocks

The Brutalist architectural style was popular in the mid-20th century, spawning from the Modernist architectural movement and flourishing from the 1950s to the mid-1970s. Examples of its style are typically very linear and blockish, often constructed out of concrete. Initially the style came about for government buildings and low-rent housing. Brutalism took the idea of unity of form and sleek futurism even further. Where Modernism embraced a sleek, simple approach to windows, for example, Brutalism went one step further by minimising or even outright eliminating them altogether!

THE BLUEPRINT

Boston City Hall – a shining example of Brutalist architecture – was voted the ugliest building in the world in 2008. And, if you've seen it, you'll know why.

Another Level

Brutalism's stark and clinical appearance is unpopular with many people, but the style was born out of necessity. Britain was rebuilding itself following the Second World War, and also undergoing a massive civic building programme to establish the Welfare State. Materials however, due to the war effort, were scarce, and costly schools and housing would have to fulfil essential functions only. The limited budget tied neatly in with Le Corbusier's fashionable philosophy of architecture, which was based on science, technology and pure function – and a huge number of buildings were created in this mode.

The 31-storey Trellick Tower, West London, UK (Ernö Goldfinger, 1966–72)

Take it to the Top!

Basically, any time you see a giant cement building with a thick, angular silhouette – that's Brutalism. Some people don't find the style in any way beautiful, but they do look cool. Especially the ones that look like they are straight out of a blockbuster sci-fi movie. Check out these futuristic-looking buildings:

Geisel Library, University of California, San Diego, USA (William Pereira, opened in 1970)

J. Edgar Hoover Building, the headquarters of the FBI, Washington DC, USA (Charles F. Murphy and Associates, 1965–75)

Klinikum Aachen or Universitätsklinikum Aachen, Germany, the biggest single-building hospital in Europe (construction started in 1972, opened in 1985)

Nichinan Cultural Center, Nichinan, Japan (Kenzo Tange, 1963)

Jatiyo Sangshad Bhaban, National Parliament House, Bangladesh (Louis Kahn, 1961–82)

Central Research Institute of Robotics and Technical Cybernetics, St. Petersburg, Russia (1973–88)

The 35-storey Western City Gate or Genex Tower, Belgrade, Serbia (Mihajlo Mitrovic, 1977)

The Cathedral of Brasilia

The world famous architect of the city of Brasilia, Oscar Niemeyer, was highly influential for his monumental buildings, sculpted from reinforced concrete. His most famous creation was the Brasilia Cathedral...

Building Blocks

In 1956, President Kubitschek of Brazil decided to build a new capital city from scratch. The new capital would be 'the most original and precise expression of creative intelligence of modern Brazil.' He commissioned Niemeyer to build Brasilia, a city that would bring about a new reality and erase the past. This was idealistic, political architecture in practice, buildings intended to change how Brazilians felt about themselves and how they were seen by the world.

Another Level

The cathedral is designed to look like a place of energetic worship. It looks rather like an erupting volcano, or arms reaching up to heaven, with a huge cross raised above it. The cathedral is what is known as a hyperboloid structure, constructed from 16 concrete columns, weighing 90 tonnes each! With nearly one million visitors per year, the cathedral is the most visited place in Brasilia.

THE BLUEPRINT

Niemeyer built a cathedral, a Congress building with a Senate and House of Representatives, a Supreme Court and many other buildings in the brand new capital, Brasilia.

'The most important thing is life. I think the young man demonstrating on the street is doing more important work than I am.'

Oscar Niemeyer

THINK OUTSIDE THE BOX In his lifetime, Niemeyer completed over 500 architectural projects – he never retired, working until his death in 2012 aged 104.

Tadao Ando

This self-taught Japanese architect has strongly influenced modern architecture. Known for his love of nothingness and empty spaces, for Ando, simplicity is magic.

Building Blocks

Ando's architectural style is calm, quiet and minimal with great attention paid to the contrast of light and shadow, the natural and the man made. His austere buildings are regarded as fine artworks, geometric forms crafted in smooth exposed concrete. The fusion of Western Modernism with Japanese building traditions set his projects in perfect harmony with the landscape. The one element carried through Tadao Ando's structures is his idolisation of the reinforced concrete wall. The importance given to walls is a distinct departure from Modernist architecture.

Awarded the Pritzker Prize in 1995

Another Level

One of Ando's finest works is Church of the Light, Osaka, which was built in 1989. A simple rectangle of smooth concrete, which is sliced through by a free-standing wall set at a 15-degree angle to the rectangle, as if the wall was a door partly open. This creates an entrance at the rear. At the far end, the wall is cut right through with a cross shape so light shines through from outside. The room appears very simple, but is a clever manipulation of space that uses light and shadow to dramatic effect. Rather like religion, the church building makes perfect sense but at the same time is unexplainable.

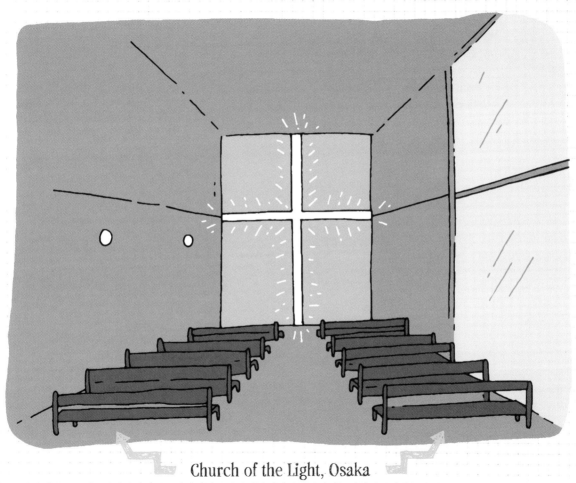

Church of the Light, Osaka

Modernism

The dominant architectural ideology of the 20th century, Modernism embraced science, technology and mass production to drive forward society's economical, cultural and technological progress. Modernist architecture is straightforward, economical and efficient.

Building Blocks

In the 1920s, architecture adapted to the machine age, following the Industrial Revolution. A rejection of tradition, paired up with Louis Sullivan's belief that 'Form Follows Function' (all designs should be derived from purpose only), led to a new wave of construction designed to improve the quality of everyday life.

Another Level

All Modernist buildings must subscribe to the Modernist manifesto of style and aesthetics. Get your pens ready to tick off the following essential components of Modernism!

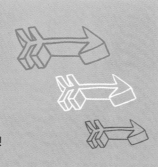

Modernist manifesto of style and aesthetics

- ✓ All buildings must follow Louis Sullivan's concept of 'form follows function'; purpose comes before looks.
- ✓ Buildings should be simple, and forego any unnecessary detail.
- ✓ Materials are to be used at 90 degrees to each other (everything should look square or rectangular).
- ✓ Buildings must showcase the materials used in the construction, instead of hiding them.
- ✓ There should be a predominant use of iron, steel, glass – all industrial, man-made materials.

Key buildings

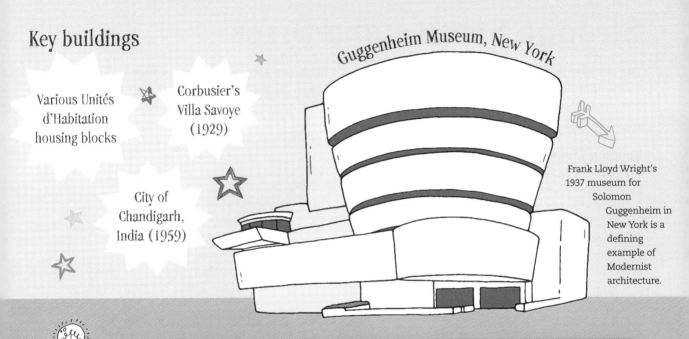

Various Unités d'Habitation housing blocks

Corbusier's Villa Savoye (1929)

City of Chandigarh, India (1959)

Guggenheim Museum, New York

Frank Lloyd Wright's 1937 museum for Solomon Guggenheim in New York is a defining example of Modernist architecture.

THINK OUTSIDE THE BOX

The Modernist style received some criticism. Flat roofs are commonly used in Modernist buildings as an architectural theme, but many critics to this day point out that a flat roof contradicts the Modernist policy of form follows function. Flat roof design is problematic: they collect rain and snow, rather than deflect like slanted roof tops.

Strange Shapes and Sizes

The world is jam-packed with architectural delights that look a million miles away from regular old buildings such as a school or library. Let us now look up to the sky in wonder at the most adventurous architecture that has ever been constructed by human hands...

Building Blocks

Architecture doesn't always have to apply itself to Louis Sullivan's idea of 'Form Follows Function'. Sometimes giant skyscrapers can look like something from an alien invasion – if that's what the architect desires. Some of the strangest-looking buildings in the world still have a purpose, they just look cool while doing it! Richard Rodgers' Georges Pompidou Centre, France, is a museum – but it doesn't look like one. Sit down and think about the type of building you'd create. How would it look?

THE BLUEPRINT

Described as the 'worst building in the history of mankind,' and 'Hotel of Doom', North Korea's Ryugyong hotel, in Pyongyang, promised to be the 'world's largest hotel,' but has still yet to open 28 years after the first concrete slab was dropped. At 105 storeys and a whopping 3,000 rooms, the pyramid-shaped hotel is constructed entirely of concrete, is taller than New York's Chrysler Building and looks like a very cool space-age rocket ship! The mega-building was meant to be a symbol of North Korea's economic strength, but the city of Pyongyang in which it resides is so poor it cannot light up the streets at night. It is now a symbol of international ridicule and will probably never open.

Take it to the Top!

While there are more than 12 strange-looking buildings in the world – hundreds more than you can ever imagine, in fact – start by finding out about the strange architectural delights of these kooky, but inspired, buildings:

Eden Project, Cornwall, UK

The Crooked House, Sopot, Poland

CCTV Headquarters, Beijing, China

Lotus Temple, Delhi, India

Kansas City Library, Missouri, USA

The Church of Hallgrimur, Reykjavik, Iceland

Kunsthaus, Graz, Austria

Atomium, Brussels, Belgium

Bibliotheca Alexandrina, Egypt

The National Library, Minsk, Belarus

House Attack, Vienna, Austria

Upside Down House, Szymbark, Poland

THINK OUTSIDE THE BOX

The 160m (525ft) tall Capital Gate building in Abu Dhabi has been certified by the *Guinness Book of World Records* as the world's furthest-leaning man-made tower. The building leans 18 degrees, four times more than the Leaning Tower of Pisa. Picture that in your mind!

Sustainable Architecture

Sustainable architecture is the future of the industry. No longer will buildings be constructed wastefully or without a concern for the environmental impact of a structure.

Building Blocks

To build a shelter, one needs to claim both land and materials from nature. Once built, we then add systems for bathing, cooking, heating and lighting. Because of this, buildings are very heavy consumers of energy, even more so than cars.

Another Level

Before the 1960s there was very little concern about finite natural resources. Everyone had signed up to Modernism's principle that technology would solve all problems. It then became obvious, through the oil crisis of 1973 and also the detection of global warming, that human beings are having a disastrous effect on the planet's health.

Take it to the Top!

Part of an architect's job in recent years has been to design buildings with minimal impact on natural resources. Green Architecture refers to buildings made from recycled or environmentally friendly materials. They may also generate power themselves, using solar panels or wind turbines. The next stage is Passive Architecture, where a building has zero impact on the environment and generates all of its own energy.

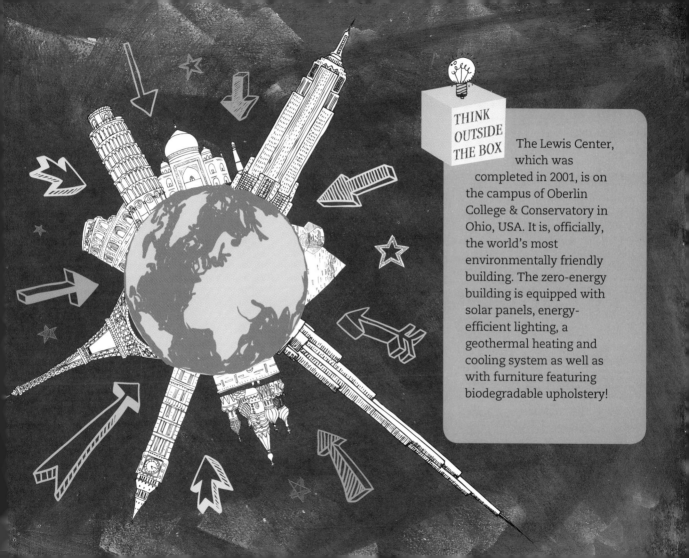

THINK OUTSIDE THE BOX

The Lewis Center, which was completed in 2001, is on the campus of Oberlin College & Conservatory in Ohio, USA. It is, officially, the world's most environmentally friendly building. The zero-energy building is equipped with solar panels, energy-efficient lighting, a geothermal heating and cooling system as well as with furniture featuring biodegradable upholstery!

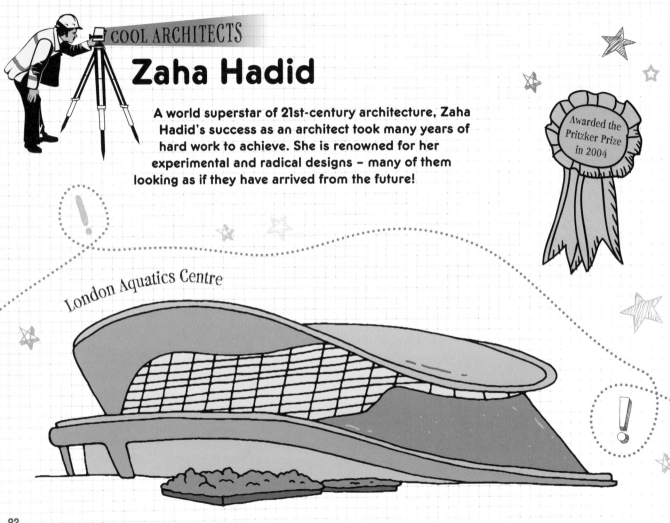

Zaha Hadid

A world superstar of 21st-century architecture, Zaha Hadid's success as an architect took many years of hard work to achieve. She is renowned for her experimental and radical designs – many of them looking as if they have arrived from the future!

Awarded the Pritzker Prize in 2004

London Aquatics Centre

Building Blocks

At first colleges and universities were much more enthusiastic about Hadid's ideas than construction companies, who found her designs too challenging. Clearly she was someone worth listening to. So Hadid spent most of her time in the 1980s teaching classes about architecture rather than building. She began to pick up awards for her designs but it took another 20 years for her to become established. She now builds cultural centres, galleries, offices and sports stadia all around the world.

Another Level

Hadid has defined a radically new approach to architecture by creating buildings, such as the Rosenthal Center for Contemporary Art in Cincinnati, with multiple perspective points and fragmented geometry to evoke the chaos of modern life. Her buildings are like science fiction!

THINK OUTSIDE THE BOX

Hadid was the first woman to receive the Pritzker prize (2004) as well as the first woman to win Designs of the Year award (2014).

Pompidou and Paris

This once controversial, and now beloved, building in the heart of Paris turned the architectural world on its head. It was a design so experimental that it was to open the doors for every architect since to think big and think differently about exterior and interior use of space.

Building Blocks

Renzo Piano and Richard Rogers won a competition in 1971 to design and build an arts centre in Paris that would 'democratise' public access to art. Piano and Rogers' winning design turned the building, and a whole lot of ideas about architecture, inside out! All of the staircases, corridors, plumbing and pipework of the Georges Pompidou Centre are on the outside of the building, maximising the public space inside, which contains a museum of contemporary art, a public library, a conference centre, children's play areas, restaurants and shops.

Another Level

Many people were critical of the design at first, calling it an 'eyesore' and 'a gerbil's cage', and referring to the architectural style as 'bowellism' – as if the intestines of an animal had been put on the outside of its body! But the effectiveness of the design has proved itself over time, and the Pompidou Centre remains one of the most visited places in Paris.

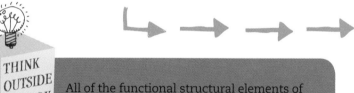

THINK OUTSIDE THE BOX   All of the functional structural elements of the centre were initially colour-coded: green pipes are plumbing, blue ducts are for climate control, electrical wires are encased in yellow, and circulation elements and devices for safety are red.

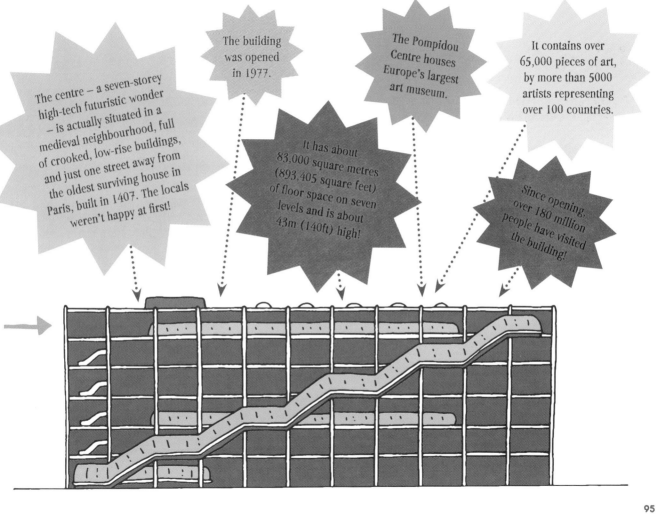

The centre – a seven-storey high-tech futuristic wonder – is actually situated in a medieval neighbourhood, full of crooked, low-rise buildings, and just one street away from the oldest surviving house in Paris, built in 1407. The locals weren't happy at first!

The building was opened in 1977.

It has about 83,000 square metres (893,405 square feet) of floor space on seven levels and is about 43m (140ft) high!

The Pompidou Centre houses Europe's largest art museum.

It contains over 65,000 pieces of art, by more than 5000 artists representing over 100 countries.

Since opening, over 180 million people have visited the building!

Disastertecture!

Buildings aren't always overnight successes. Sometimes they are disliked by the critics and people alike. Sometimes they fall down when they shouldn't and sometimes they fall famously out of fashion.

Building Blocks

Architects have to have strong skins – and so do their buildings. A building's design can fall out of use in two ways:

It no longer serves a purpose for people.	OR	There is no will to keep using it. Either the building fails us, or we fail the building.

What remains, if not reused, becomes a ruin, a physical symbol of the idea that nothing lasts forever.

Many ancient buildings – places of architecture that once had a purpose – are now ruins. They don't *do* anything except stand as historical fragments, but many are visited by millions of people each year. Their purpose has changed – which is better than being torn down.

Another Level

Sometimes buildings and works of radical architecture are hated at first and then, slowly but surely, become loved. Take the Eiffel Tower, for example.

It was built by the French architect Gustave Eiffel in 1889 to celebrate the centennial of the French Revolution and to serve as a symbol of France's industrial strength. Its construction took two years, two months and five days and, at the time, was a technical and architectural achievement. Gustave's plan was to build the highest tower in the world – a lattice of girders made of pure iron, anchored by four piers. The locals hated the idea! They wanted something more natural-looking. As construction of the tower progressed, nervous Parisians feared that the tower would attract lightning, or fall over onto their homes! It hasn't yet. Only intended to last 20 years, the tower has now stood proud for over a century and is the most visited monument you have to pay to see in the world!

Take it to the Top!

Las Vegas lies deep in the deserts of Nevada and the city's best 'hotspot' is literally that! Known as Death Ray Hotel, the beautiful-looking Vdara hotel is an architectural marvel and one of Las Vegas's most popular places. Unfortunately, this exotic glass skyscraper has had guests complain of receiving severe burns from a 'death ray' of sunlight caused by the unique design of the building – the building's windows magnify and reflect the sun's rays onto an area of the swimming pool at temperatures hot enough to singe hair or melt plastic! The phenomenon occurs when intense heat is created by the curved glass surface of the hotel, which acts as a parabolic dish. The glass bounces the rays from the sun and concentrates the light in a 4.5m × 3m (15ft × 10ft) hot zone on a portion of the pool deck. The architects thought they had solved the problem by installing a high-tech film on the hotel's glass windows to reduce the effect, but that did not solve the problem entirely.

Due to the changing of the seasons and the Earth's rotation, the position of the hotel's hotspot changes every day.

How would **you** fix this 'death ray' problem?

Postmodernism

When it comes to Postmodernism just remember one thing:

Anything Goes!

Building Blocks

Postmodernism is a fusion of many different styles and methods. It combines new with old in whatever way the architect feels will work the best. Rather like sampling in music, Postmodern architects borrow inspiration from wherever they like to compose their buildings. Keep a look out for Postmodern buildings as you go about your business today.

Another Level

Postmodernism was (and is) a movement that was a reaction in the 1970s and 1980s to the purist period of 'Less Is More' functionalism that had followed the Second World War. In fact, many Postmodern architects adopted the motto – Less is Bore!

After the 1960s, people were ready to start having fun again, to be less serious about everything. The results are witty, eccentric buildings that are brand new, but often reference previous eras. Ornamentation could be for ironic purposes, or a modern-looking building would have a classical rooftop.

FAMOUS POSTMODERN BUILDINGS

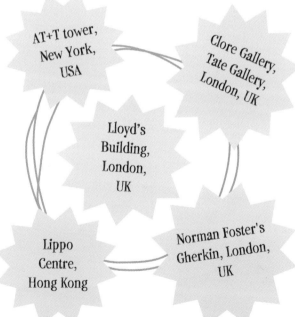

AT+T tower, New York, USA

Clore Gallery, Tate Gallery, London, UK

Lloyd's Building, London, UK

Lippo Centre, Hong Kong

Norman Foster's Gherkin, London, UK

Postmodern architecture combines functionality with aesthetics in a way that had never been done before in past architectural movements.

Postmodern architects can feel free to add unexpected touches to their buildings that go against convention but still look good to the eye.

Use any colours you want, but stick within a colour scheme.

High five!

'If there's no cake, what do you do with the icing?' – a common Postmodern architect's saying.

If you want your building to look like a robot – go for it!

The Guggenheim, Bilbao

Built in four years, from 1993 to 1997, the Guggenheim Museum in Bilbao, Spain is a perfect example of Deconstructivism and is a building that also put the city firmly onto the global tourism map.

Building Blocks

Dramatic and unforgettable, the Guggenheim Museum looks rather like a huge car crash, or a pile of dented tin cans. But what looks like a huge messy accident is actually a very carefully designed structure. The only way to design a building like this is to use computers to calculate stability, strength and weight distribution.

This unlikely building was made by the Canadian architect Frank Gehry.
Style: Deconstructivism

The Bilbao Guggenheim measures 24,000 square metres (258,000 square feet)!

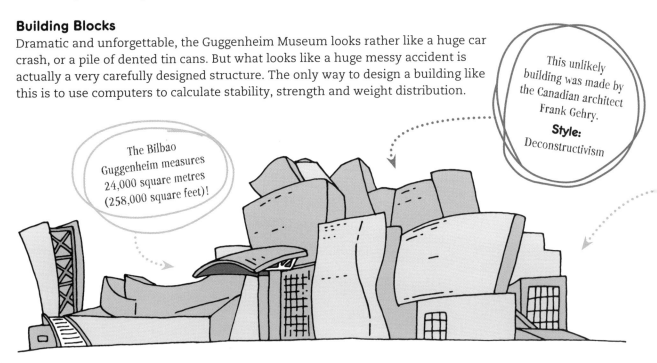

Another Level

The museum's architect, Frank Gehry, has been criticised for just making disorganised, irregular shapes that are visual artworks rather than spaces that have a function. Some of his buildings are also structurally weak and have to be repaired or modified shortly after completion, suggesting his work is more about style than substance. All of this makes him rather unpopular among serious form-follows-function architects.

Take it to the Top!

Famously, Gehry once designed a building by taking a sheet of paper, crumpling it up in his hand, and declaring it to be an architectural model.

It is difficult to tell which walls support the main structure, which is typical of the Deconstructivist style, where buildings look broken and as if they defy gravity.

THINK OUTSIDE THE BOX

The Bilbao Effect

Whatever the critics' opinions of Gehry's design, the building changed the fortunes of Bilbao, the city becoming a major international tourist attraction overnight. Other, smaller cities around the world now also wanted a similar building for themselves and a boom in city officials commissioning very famous architects to build highly eccentric looking galleries began. This is known as the Bilbao Effect, and has produced some very mixed results! Similar attempts elsewhere have failed and are running up huge losses. Two ambitious projects in the UK, the Sheffield Centre for Popular Music by Nigel Coates, and Will Alsop's The Public at West Bromwich, have been closed down. In Spain, Santiago's City of Arts in Valencia is incomplete, struggling and vastly over budget. Even one of Gehry's own projects, the Ohr-O'Keefe Museum of Art in Biloxi, Mississippi, USA, has only been able to open one of the five new buildings.

Design Your Own Home

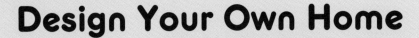

The house you are, no doubt, sitting in right at this very second is an architectural wonder that is built upon thousands of years of architectural history. Let's find out more about the humble house...

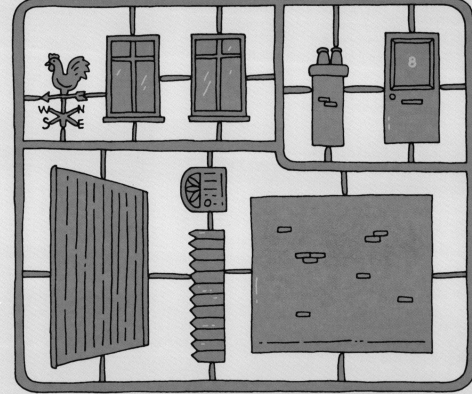

Building Blocks

When discussing architecture, it can be easy to overlook the most popular type of architecture anywhere in the world – your house. If you could live anywhere in the world, where would you go? And what would your house look like? What features would you incorporate to make it the coolest house ever?

Another Level

Modern houses often get criticised for looking the same – they don't have many outstanding architectural features. But in and of themselves they are unique. Take a walk around the house you live in. Walk into each room and observe the corners of the wall, the shape and size of the room and any strange features, look at the floors and the ceilings and make notes on your findings. Look at the house from the outside. Once you've got a picture of how your house is structured, design a floor plan of it, like the one on this page.

THINK OUTSIDE THE BOX

Used for thousands of years, bricks are known among masonry experts as the most eco-friendly materials available for construction. The most common bricks are made from clay after they are heated at 1000 degrees Celsius! An average sized three-bedroom house requires around 16,000 bricks. That's nothing – around 3.8 billion bricks were used to build the Great Wall of China!

The Shard

The Shard is the newest addition to London's iconic skyline. It's also the city's tallest building. Oh wait, hang on. It's now also the tallest building in Europe – but still only the 59th tallest building in the world.

Building Blocks

The name 'Shard' derives from the sculpted glass design, made up of tapering glass facets that do not meet at the top. The top looks like jagged shards of glass. The effect is that of a sharp icicle shooting up into the air.

Another Level

A steel structure is built around a central concrete core. This makes such a tall building very stable but also surprisingly flexible – the frame allows the building to sway side-to-side by up to 50cm (19in) in high winds.

Take it to the Top!

Over four decades, Italian architect Renzo Piano has established a reputation as one of the world's greatest design innovators. For The Shard, he drew inspiration from the history of the local area, from the tall sailing ships that once filled the docks, to the tall spires of Christopher Wren's city churches.

The Shard is 309.6m (1,016 ft) high.

95 per cent of the construction materials are recycled.

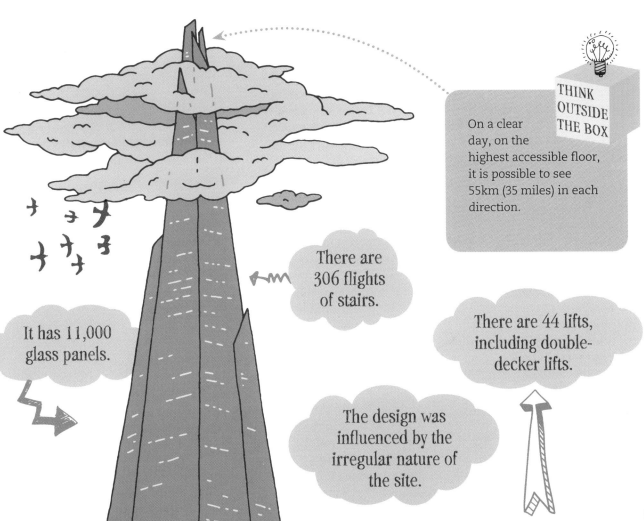

THINK OUTSIDE THE BOX

On a clear day, on the highest accessible floor, it is possible to see 55km (35 miles) in each direction.

There are 306 flights of stairs.

It has 11,000 glass panels.

There are 44 lifts, including double-decker lifts.

The design was influenced by the irregular nature of the site.

Architecture and Control

How does an architect make sure a place is open to everyone but also safe and secure? Preventing crime and keeping people safe while also allowing free access and movement is a commonplace challenge for designers and urban planners. Many tricks of this trade, often known as architecture of control, are cleverly designed to be unnoticed by an untrained eye. Let's see if we can spot some!

Building Blocks

Architects can direct people's movement easily enough by positioning walls and pathways that intentionally send people to (or away from!) a particular location. More sophisticated examples of control include positioning the windows in school classrooms high up the wall so seated pupils can't gaze out of the window when they are supposed to be studying! Do you think this is fair? Do you think that it is right or wrong to control people by design? Let's look at some other examples of how we are controlled by architects.

Another Level

Where benches, seats and trees are not quite what they seem! Designing spaces that control behaviour is more efficient than having to constantly monitor people in case they misbehave. It is also best to prevent crimes from happening in the first place, rather than having to chase and arrest people. Here are some examples:

Speed humps

Often called 'sleeping policemen' not because policemen tend to be fat, lazy and often found lying in the road, but because each hump keeps the traffic speed down, so the policeman's job is done for him by the architect!

Park benches

The park-keeper likes park benches because visitors can sit down, rest, and take in the view. The park-keeper's problem is that homeless people keep using the benches to sleep on, stopping other people from using them. The solution? A handrail is added to the middle of the bench, which allows people to sit, but not lie down. Many parks and public squares now have seating that stops people from lying down. The park-keeper is happy, but where does the homeless man sleep now?

Seats in bus stops

You may have noticed how seating in bus-stops now consists of a very narrow shelf that tilts downward at the front. This design means that users still have to support themselves with their feet and the seat is uncomfortable. The aim is to stop people loitering in bus stops, which might be a good idea, but not so good if you are tired and the bus is late!

Seating in shopping centres

If not removed entirely, public seating in shopping centres is deliberately designed to be uncomfortable. A bench will usually have a hump in the seat and a backrest at a steep angle, deliberately designed so that users only sit there for a few minutes before standing up and doing more shopping. No time to rest when the shops are open!

Anti-skateboarding studs

Have you noticed these shiny metal studs protruding from low walls in public squares? They aren't decoration, they stop skaters sliding along the walls. Are the skateboarders really a nuisance or does public space belong to them as much as anyone else?

CCTV Trees

Nature has a soothing effect on people: Richard Rogers has a design policy guaranteeing that whichever window in one of his buildings you look out from, you will always be able to see a tree. For the police, however, trees are problematic, because they can conceal criminal activity. New trees planted in city centre squares are now chosen with CCTV in mind. The trunks should be very slender and rise over 1.8m (6ft) before branching out so everyone remains visible on camera.

There's only one way in here!

The Future of Architecture

Becoming an architect means being able to look into the future – being a visionary of not only space but of time too! You have to design your building not only for the present, but you'll also have to travel in time and work out what your building could be used for in 10, 20 and 100 years from now. Architecture has travelled far and ventured wide over the past few thousand years of human development and civilisation. One thing is for sure: it looks like the future will look very cool indeed!

Building Blocks

In 2010, for the first time in history, it was recorded that the majority of the world's population (54 per cent) lived in cities, and this percentage will only continue to grow. One hundred years ago, two out of every 10 people lived in an urban area. By 2050, this will increase to seven out of 10 people. What this means for architects of the future is that they will have to build upwards to fit everyone in. But what other types of cool architecture of the future can we expect?

Rotating Skyscrapers

In the future, not everybody will be able to afford to live in the penthouse apartment of a tall building with the best views. But that's OK, dynamic architects are bringing the view to you! The Dynamic Tower currently being built in Dubai is a 420m (1,378ft) tall skyscraper with 80 floors that independently rotate around every 90 minutes – this means no matter what floor you're on, your view of the world will always be changing!

Invisible Skyscrapers

The Tower Infinity, a planned 450m (1476ft) skyscraper just outside Seoul, South Korea is to become the world's first skyscraper that is intended to appear invisible! The skyscraper will contain tiny cameras that will capture and project real-time images of the city's surroundings, which will then be displayed on hundreds of rows of LED screens spread all across the tower. By building an invisible tower, architects have promised that observers will be able to see the city's sights that normally such a huge building would block.

One of the best
examples of the
Futurism architectural
movement is the Cayan Tower,
Dubai, a 306m (1004ft) 80-floor
mega building... with a twist.
Literally! It is the highest
building in the world with a
twist of 90 degrees. It looks like
a huge helix of DNA – it has to
be seen to be believed!

THE BLUEPRINT

One of the best jobs to have in the architectural world of the future
is 'Architectural technologist'. These clever people are specialists
in the science of architecture, building design and construction.
They work closely with architects and turn the architect's concept
into reality in the completed construction. They are concerned with
the technical side of design and ensure that an attractive functional
building also can operate successfully. They also make sure the
right materials are used and that building regulations are met too.
They have to have expert knowledge of the very pinnacle of future
materials so that buildings of today look and act like buildings of
tomorrow. Sounds cool, doesn't it?

What features would you design for
your building of the future?

109

Glossary

Arabesque
A decorative style that weaves together foliage in a pattern, often seen on walls and tiles in Islamic art. Often used in architecture to decorate buildings.

Basilica
Developed from Roman times, this type of church has a high central nave and lower side aisles. It was the preferred architectural style of the Christian church up until the nineteenth century.

Crenellation
Walls built around the top of a castle with regular gaps for soldiers to shoot arrows at the enemy.

Dwarf gallery
A small series of arches just below the roof of a church, a decoration typically seen in Romanesque architecture.

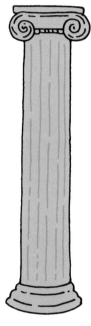

Entablature
The horizontal structure lying above the columns and below the roof in temples, often decorated with friezes.

Facade
The front exterior face of a building.

Genius Loci
Literally means 'genius of place'. Describes locations that are memorable for their affecting architectural quality.

Junk Space
A term coined by architect Rem Koolhaas describing the bland similarity of large urban buildings such as shopping centres.

Minaret
A tower associated with a mosque, used to call the faithful to prayer.

Niche
A recess in a wall, usually for holding a sculpture.

Parti

The central idea that drives an architectural work. Derived from French *partir*, meaning 'to depart to a destination.'

Quadrangle

A four-sided courtyard, often found in schools. Can be surrounded by walkways and pillars.

Render

Also known as stucco, this cement mix is used to cover walls, giving a smooth and waterproof finish.

Squinch

The filling between a domed roof and the building beneath.

Utopians

People who work on projects intended to improve society. Usually they work on ideas not yet achievable in reality. Architects do this a lot!

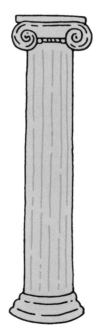

Vernacular

Like an accent, the vernacular in architecture is specific to the locality where it is found. It will have developed over a long period in one place, using materials and methods from the area.

Ziggurat

A stepped pyramid. They can be found in Central America and Mesopotamia. Invented before the pyramids in Egypt.

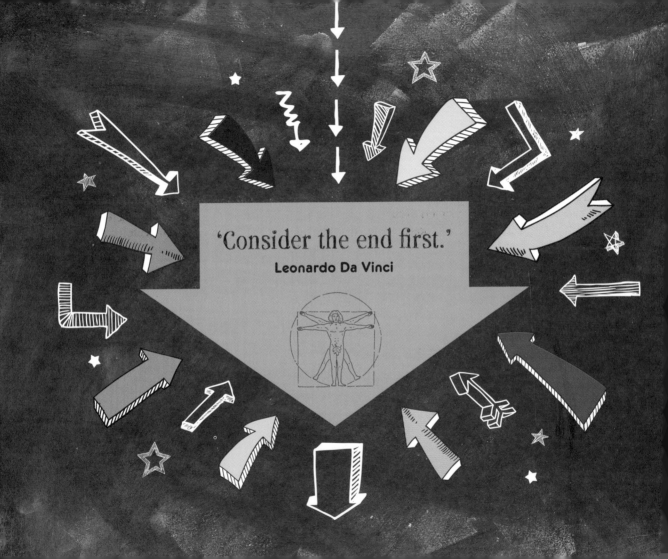

'Consider the end first.'

Leonardo Da Vinci

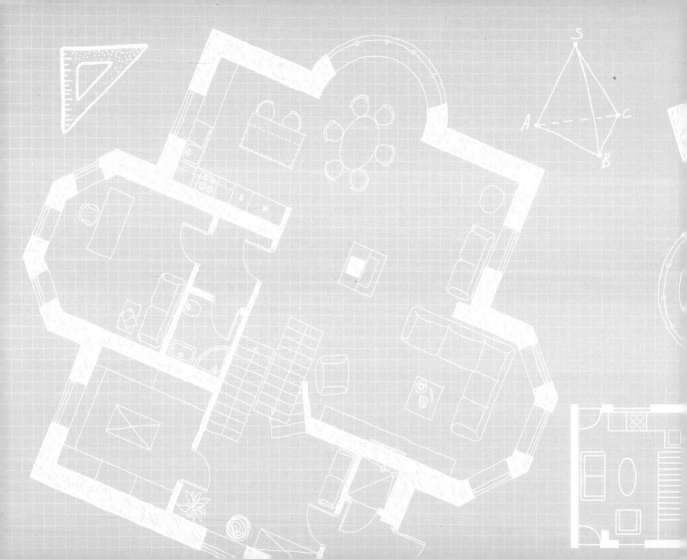